At Home in School
Parent participation in Primary Education

Viv Edwards

and

Angela Redfern

Routledge
London and New York

First published in 1988 by Routledge
11 New Fetter Lane, London EC4P 4EE
29 West 35th Street, New York NY 10001

Printed in Great Britain by Billing & Sons Ltd, Worcester

British Library Cataloguing in Publication Data
Edwards, Viv
   At home in school : parent participation
in primary education.
   1.   England. Primary schools. School life.
Participation of parents
   I.   Title   II. Redfern, Angela
   372.11'03

                              0027893

Library of Congress Cataloging in Publication Data
Edwards, Viv.
   At home in school : parent participation in primary education /
Viv Edwards, Angela Redfern.
      p. cm.
   Bibliography: p.
   Includes index.
   1. Home and school—Great Britain—Case studies.   2. Education,
Elementary—Great Britain—Case studies.   3. Education—Great
Britain—Parent participation—Case studies.   I. Redfern, Angela.
II. Title.
   LC225.33.G7E38   1988
   370.19'31'0941—dc 19   88–14864

ISBN 0–415–01294–5

                              370.34
                               EDW

                          140459

To and from Redlands

Contents

Acknowledgements

This book is based largely on Redlands Primary School, Reading. We have depended heavily on the co-operation and encouragement of the present headteacher, Mary Martyn-Johns, and the staff of the school. To ensure that all sections of the school community were represented in the book, we extended an open invitation to parents to offer comments on aspects of school life; we also sought out children's perceptions. We very much appreciated the warmth and enthusiasm of the response. It would be inappropriate to single out individuals: we are grateful to them all.

Thanks are also due to people who did not contribute directly to the writing of this book, but who have none the less played an important part in the development of our own thinking. Most important among these are former colleagues and friends Linda Cushine, Paula Gourlay, Michael Richards, John Shearman and Jill Wade; and Hilda Bateson, a former teacher who used a very different approach from the one we are describing in this book, but who very successfully engendered the interest in education which led to its writing. Grateful thanks to the Goldsmiths' Society for their Teachers' Travel Award.

We would like to thank the people who read various drafts of the book and offered comments that were both challenging and constructive: Mary Fuller, Monica Hughes, Jill Lake, Mary Martyn-Johns, Chris Morriss, Tim O'Grady, Woll Redfern, and Rani Sharma. Responsibility for the final product remains, of course, with us.

Last, but not least, our long-suffering families deserve a special mention. Thank you Woll, Kate and Sam, Edna and Jack; Chris, Dafydd, Ceri and Siân, Tom and Hett.

Authors' Note

The terminological confusion surrounding the use of 'parents' is something which needs to be recognized from the outset in a book of this kind. We would like to make it clear that our understanding of 'parents' is much broader than the traditional concept of the two-parent nuclear family: we use the term as a convenient shorthand for the very wide range of family patterns which make up any school community.

Chapter 1

Introduction

Working through the literature on the history of home-school relations can sometimes seem a little like dipping into *The Odyssey*. The pages are full of myths of epic proportions: working-class children underachieve because their parents do not talk to them enough or prepare them properly for school; only middle-class parents are interested in their children's schooling; teachers are the only people equipped to deal with the core curriculum. There are also some epic confrontations: parent groups requiring greater accountability from schools; teachers involving parents from all backgrounds in the teaching of reading and other activities which have traditionally been the preserve of 'professionals', in spite of opposition from teachers' unions and more conservative colleagues.

The last twenty years have been very exciting times for teachers and parents alike. They have seen the gradual move from the total separation of home and school to an increasing acceptance of the central role of parents as partners in their children's education. We are dealing, of course, with a dynamic situation where some schools and teachers have gone considerably further down the road to partnership than others. But the general direction of this movement is now firmly established.

For the last eight years, one of us, Angela Redfern, has worked as deputy head and the other, Viv Edwards, has been a parent at Redlands Primary School, Reading. The starting-point for this book was the feeling that Redlands had made a good deal of progress towards partnership with parents. We had just given a talk to a group of teachers on a course at Reading University on 'The Community as a Resource of Reading', based mainly on our experience at Redlands, and had been taken aback by the responses of some of the people taking part. Certain course members absolved themselves of responsibility for thinking seriously about involving parents, either by blaming the management: 'Yes, this is an interesting idea, but I could never get my head to go along with it', or by blaming the parents: 'The parents in our school just aren't interested in their children's education'. One man dismissed the relevance of what we were talking about for his school because Redlands is an inner-city school with a high proportion of ethnic minority children: 'I can see why you'd need to do that in a school with lots of immigrants, but we've only got two Chinese in our school'!

Our own very positive experience of joint ventures with parents at Redlands made us sure of our ground. All parents, irrespective of their background are interested in their children's education and, given the opportunity and encouragement to become involved in school life, respond enthusiastically. Each new experiment strengthened our basic belief that parental involvement was very good for the children and that both teachers and parents gained a lot through working together. Maybe it would be useful to share our experience with others . . .

Writing for a mixed audience

Parental involvement in schools is a recent development. Yet the number of books with titles such as *Parents, Teachers and Children* or *Parents as Partners* bears witness to the remarkable growth of interest in this area. Many of these books are purely academic accounts which focus on the theoretical rather than the practical implications of parent participation. Some are books written exclusively for teachers and are essentially guides as to the advantages and pitfalls of working more closely with parents and how this can be achieved. Others concentrate on just one area of involvement which, in most cases, is reading.

We wanted to write a very different kind of book. We envisage that our audience will in the main be student teachers and practising teachers who are interested in looking more closely at the issue of parental involvement. However, we are also conscious of the increasing numbers of parents who are eager to broaden their knowledge of their children's schooling and are receptive to any ideas on how they can co-operate more closely with teachers. We therefore felt it was important to write an account which was accessible to both groups of potential readers.

We believe that ours is a success story in that we have moved a long way – and indeed are still moving – towards a genuine and meaningful parent-teacher partnership and are very aware of the benefits for all concerned. However, we have no illusions about the many shortcomings which we have yet to tackle. We know that what is taking place in Redlands is considerably in advance of what has happened in some places, but we also recognize that we have a great deal to learn from many other initiatives elsewhere. Our aim is thus not to present a picture of complacency; rather, we want to show how we have tried to cope with both failure and success. We want to provide a practical account to which both teachers and parents will be able to relate.

How the book is organized

We have approached this task in a number of different ways. First, we felt it was important to provide a national context for developments at Redlands. The disadvantage of describing what has happened in one school is that it tends to focus on the specific. Issues which have attracted national attention may or may not have been matters of concern in Redlands. Similarly, things that have happened in Redlands may or may not be relevant to teachers and parents in other schools. For this reason the first part of this book takes the form of a brief history of parents and school which forms the backcloth for the account of Redlands which follows.

It starts in chapter 2 with a description of attitudes towards parents in the first half of the century and the prevailing philosophy of education which placed parents in a marginal rather than a central role. The Plowden Report on *Children and their Primary Schools* (1967) is discussed at length, because of its enormous impact on teachers' perception of parents and its importance in sanctioning parental involvement in their children's schooling.

In chapter 3 we describe the ways in which the basic recommendations of Plowden – the formation of parent-teacher associations, the opening of the school to parents and the establishment of better communications with parents – were gradually implemented. We also look at how the more recent 1980 and 1986 Education Acts have made some of the Plowden recommendations legal requirements, and have helped to develop the notion that schools should be accountable to parents.

Schools can involve parents in their children's formal education in many different ways. They can help to raise funds by joining a parent-teacher association; they can attend meetings for new parents or parent evenings; they can be invited to school plays and other special events. Yet none of these activities necessarily involves parents in the daily life of the school.

In chapter 4 we look more closely at initiatives which have drawn on the help of parents both at home and in school, both in often undervalued areas such as cooking and sewing and in core-curriculum subjects such as reading and writing. We examine the question of the expert status of teachers and the ability of parents to handle spheres of activity which have been the traditional territory of the teacher. We conclude that there is an inevitable – and very healthy – move towards recognizing parents as equal and complementary partners in their children's education.

Part 2 is a description of the way in which one school, Redlands Primary, has gradually moved towards this partnership with parents. The main focus for this part of the book is Angela Redfern's personal account of what it has been like to be a teacher during this period of change. It starts in chapter 5 with a description of life in an inner-city school in the 1970s. The writer started her career as a primary teacher in this school just before the arrival of a new headteacher who believed passionately in the need for parents to play an active part in their children's schooling. This was a period of rapid change in which teachers were grappling with the basic challenges of Plowden and looking at ways in which parents – and community – could become more fully involved in the life of the school.

We move in chapter 6 to Redlands where the writer took up a post as deputy head in 1980. Again, by coincidence, there was a new headteacher. Both the head and the deputy head had come from schools which had begun to involve parents and were keen to introduce change to their new school. The rest of the book examines the various stages which were involved in this process of change.

The chapters in this second part of the book loosely follow the order in which changes took place, for instance, the development of the Parent-Teacher Association (chapter 6), the policy of open access (chapter 7) and the appointment of parent governors (chapter 8), and were well under way before parents became involved as classroom helpers (chapter 9) or in the core curriculum (chapter 10). But while parental involvement in Redlands and elsewhere would seem to have passed through a number of different stages, it is not simply a matter of going from one discrete stage to another. For instance, the formation of parent-teacher associations was one of the earlier forms of parental involvement. But whereas many schools have gone on to explore other forms of co-operation, the form and function of the PTA has neither disappeared nor stood still. Each chapter thus deals with a particular kind of involvement and tries to chart its progress over a period of time.

Finally, in chapter 11, we take the opportunity to reflect on what has happened in Redlands over the last seven years: what lessons have we learnt? What issues do we need to consider more carefully? We also try to generalize from our experience. Why do some schools look more favourably on parental involvement than others? What are the best ways of encouraging parent participation in schools?

Parents and children?

In the final analysis, partnership with parents affects three different groups of people: teachers, parents and children. For this reason, we felt it was important that the teacher perspective on change should not stand alone. We invited comments from both parents and children at Redlands. Over half the families in the school responded and their views have duly been recorded.

We are well aware of possible criticisms of collecting data in this way. Parents and children may have felt duty bound to give us the answers which they believed we were expecting: we might have built up a more reliable picture if they had been interviewed by an outsider. However, there is a well-established tradition in the school of parents offering honest feedback on developments, and, for this reason, parents could be confident that all comments – critical as well as complementary – would be welcomed. We were able to talk freely and at length to a very wide range of people with whom we have a close and good working relationship. They expressed criticisms and frustrations as well as encouragement and approval, and we have no reason to believe that what they told us was not a true reflection of what they actually felt.

How representative are these comments of the school as a whole? It would have been an easy matter, for instance, to have talked only to those parents whom we felt were in tune with our way of thinking. As it happened, the families who responded came from the whole range of social and ethnic groups represented in the school. Their observations on all aspects of involvement in school have been placed at the end of the appropriate chapters. We have organized them thematically but, because we feel it is important that people should be allowed to speak for themselves, we have offered no commentary.

Together, the teacher account and the parents' and children's comments constitute a full record of the main developments in relationships with parents in one primary school over a seven-year period from 1980 to 1987. Redlands is a Primary School with 222 children currently on its roll. The school population draws on a very wide range of social and ethnic groups – English families who have lived in the area for several generations; families who came from the Indian subcontinent and the Caribbean whose children have been born in Britain; temporary residents in bed and breakfast accommodation; the children of doctors working permanently or on short-term contracts at the hospital; university families and postgraduate students from overseas. A very high proportion of parents work either part- or full-time and this includes the mothers as well as the fathers. Many are shiftworkers at the hospital or in factories. Children at the school speak a total of twenty-three different languages between them.

There is a high turnover of children in the school, not only because of the bed and breakfast, university and hospital families who move on, but because of the nature of the housing stock close to the school. There is a high proportion of small terraced houses which attract first-time buyers. Very often, as children reach the junior stage, their parents move to more spacious accommodation outside the catchment area, and as a result the bulk of the school population is found in the Infant department.

As it happens, Redlands is an inner-city school which draws on a racially and linguistically diverse population of children. It is our observation that some of the most innovative work involving parents has taken place in schools like ours. Early difficulties in communication made it important for parents and teachers to search for common ground and one of the obvious ways forward was to involve the children's family in the life of the school. The presence of ethnic minority children has often served as a catalyst for helping teachers think about the broader implications of parent involvement. However, we have not set out to write a book on multi-racial schools. We believe that the developments which are taking place in schools like ours are of importance for all schools, irrespective of their social class or ethnic composition.

Part One

Parents and school – a brief history

Chapter 2

Parents: help or hindrance?

The publication in 1967 of the Plowden Report, *Children and their Primary Schools*,[1] was such an important turning-point in home-school relations that all developments since that time can be seen as relating either directly to the Report or to the lively debate which followed in its wake. For the first time, there was official recognition of the potential role which parents could play in their children's schooling. The Report drew on a great deal of research on the relationship between home background and educational achievement. It faithfully mirrored the growing number of initiatives by teachers to narrow the distance between home and school. Inevitably, it also drew on many aspects of the conventional wisdom of the day which were subsequently questioned and found to be lacking. In this chapter, we will look critically at the attitudes towards parents which led to, and informed, Plowden.

No parents beyond this point

We have travelled a long way in our ideas of what school is all about. For many years education was the exclusive domain of teachers. Ever since Plato there had been a strong belief that education should be carried out far from the interference of parents and there was no challenge to the view that teaching should be carried out behind closed doors. Gates were shut after the register had been called, visitors were actively discouraged and very few people other than officials were allowed to enter when school was in progress. The division between home and school was a very clear one, marked symbolically by the white line in the playground which parents were not expected to cross.

It is easy to understand why parents were not involved in their children's education for so many years. School was seen as a means of compensating for what was lacking in the home, whether it be basic skills to ensure children's survival in a literate world or, later, free meals to ensure that their diet was adequate. Because teachers saw themselves as compensating for the deficiencies of parents, it is not surprising that parents were so totally excluded from their children's education.

There were, of course, important exceptions to this way of thinking.[2] There is evidence, for instance, that as early as the 1920s, some nursery schools held weekly clubs attended by as many as 60–70 parents. A little later in the 1930s, the Home and School Council of Great Britain broke new ground, inviting parents into school to see how their children worked. By and large, though, the position remained unchanged for many years. There was a great physical and philosophical divide between the two main educative forces in children's lives: home and school.

The 1944 Education Act

Ever since the introduction of compulsory primary education in the 1870s, school had been seen as the panacea for all ills. It was widely assumed that as soon as the masses were adequately educated many of the social problems of the day would disappear. Until the mid-1940s large numbers of children were denied a secondary education because their parents could not afford it. The 1944 Education Act was designed to be a great democratizing force, making secondary education available to all for the first time. It was widely assumed that the Act would play an important part in bringing about change and greater social justice.

The educational provision made in the wake of the 1944 Act was informed by the received wisdom of the time that intellectual ability was genetically determined. A tripartite system of grammar, secondary modern and technical schools would allow all children to achieve their educational potential. Yet, by the late 1950s, the inadequacies of this system were becoming clear. There was a growing awareness that, despite the fact that education was now compulsory and universal, not all children were benefiting from it to the same extent. Concern was being expressed both at the uneven distribution of grammar schools through the country and the fact that middle-class children were obtaining a far larger proportion of grammar school places than their working-class peers.

Attempts to explain the failure of the 1944 Act were based on the same pathological model which featured so prominently in the early years of this century. Stress was placed on the inadequacies of working-class families and their inability to provide the kind of intellectual environment which was essential for academic success. Value-laden expressions such as 'disadvantage', 'cultural and linguistic deprivation' and 'compensatory education' became clearly established in the educational vocabulary of the day. The task of the school was to compensate for the disadvantage which working-class children experienced and one of the ways in which this could be done was to educate their parents.

It was now argued, for instance, that the major determinants of educational success were social circumstances, motivation, the family and home, rather than teachers and the curriculum.[3] It was suggested that parents help the learning style of their children by passing on confidence not through knowledge but by attitudes.[4] Throughout the 1960s an increasing body of research began to suggest that parents might well have the ability to help children not only in the short term but with long-lasting results.[5]

The myth of verbal deprivation

A great deal of attention in the debate on the adequacy or otherwise of working-class families was placed on the language which they used with their children. The major impetus for this discussion was the work of Basil Bernstein[6] who postulated two polar language codes – the 'elaborated' and the 'restricted' codes. In the light of the evidence that working-class children were less likely to do well at all stages of education, he argued that the different distribution of these two codes was a possible major cause. Bernstein's work was widely interpreted as suggesting that standard English could be equated with the elaborated code and non-standard working-class dialects with the restricted code. Bernstein himself has strongly denied that this was ever his intention, but his denials did not prevent this equation becoming widely accepted by teachers.

Bernstein's work or, more correctly, the misinterpretation of his work, continues to inform popular opinion on working-class speech. The 1975 Bullock Report,[7] for instance, advocates that health visitors should urge parents to 'bathe their children in language'. Five years later, a project was set up in the Ladywood area of Birmingham involving health visitors, speech therapists and social workers.[8] Contact was made with mothers in supermarkets and workers distributed children with 'Mum, talk to me' stickers. The rationale for this scheme was that inner-city children were simply not being spoken to enough by their parents in their vital early years. As late as 1985, writers such as Tough[9] talk in stereotypical terms of homes where children do not engage in discussion with adults and ask them questions only when seeking permission.

The Bernsteinian stance has attracted bitter criticism from many different writers who hold that, while differences undoubtedly exist between working- and middle-class speech, they need not in any way support the notion of a linguistic deficit. It has been argued, for instance, that Bernstein's theory of language codes is both untestable and unrelated to linguistic evidence.[10] It has also been suggested that Bernstein has failed to take into consideration the effect which situation can have on children's speech. Children who can appear 'non-verbal' or uncommunicative in formal situations like school can be shown to be normal, fluent speakers in other less stressful situations.[11]

Much recent research by writers such as Wells[12] and Tizard and Hughes[13] has shown that the main differences in language use occur not between middle- and working-class children but between home and school. At home conversations are frequently longer and more equally balanced between adult and child. Children ask more questions and spend more time in conversation with adults. Parents play much more with their children, talk to them much more and answer many more questions than do teachers. The notion embodied in the Bullock Report and elsewhere that professionals should offer advice and suggestions to parents on how to talk to their children is seriously challenged by research findings of this kind.

A changing population

Throughout its history, British society has never been either monolingual or monocultural. However, population changes on an unprecedented scale took place during the 1950s and 1960s. The postwar period was a time of rapid economic expansion. The higher paid industrial jobs tended to be filled by English workers. Physically demanding jobs with low pay and anti-social hours became increasingly unattractive, creating a vacuum which was filled by immigrant labour. In response to advertising campaigns conducted by employers like London Transport and the National Health Service, large numbers of British citizens from the New Commonwealth – mainly the Indian subcontinent and the Caribbean – came to settle in Britain.

It was unfortunate that immigrant settlement came at a time when deficit views of working-class life and language were popular. The 'disadvantaged' label was rapidly extended to West Indian and Asian children. Language understandably formed an important focus for discussion. But, rather than starting from an appreciation of the linguistic skills which these children already had, teachers were wholly concerned with what they lacked, namely the ability to speak standard English. West Indians, speaking various Caribbean creoles, with mainly English vocabulary but often quite distinct grammars, were treated with particular scorn. Their language has been described variously as 'babyish', 'careless and slovenly', 'lacking proper grammar', and 'very relaxed like the way they walk'. Remarks on this subject made by the National Association of School Masters were particularly revealing. They refer to West Indian language as a kind 'of plantation English which is socially unacceptable and inadequate for communication'.[14]

The languages of Asian children scarcely fared any better. For many years their mother tongues were totally excluded from schools. It is perhaps not surprising that when the prevailing model in education was a deficit model, there should be no acknowledgement or understanding of the importance of the language of the home, either in identity formation or in conceptual development. There have been reports of children who have been told to stop 'jabbering' in their mother tongue in the playground.[15] And as one headteacher, consulted as part of a survey on LEA provision for immigrant children, commented: 'The Community Relations Officer thinks we should be teaching Gujarati but we couldn't start that caper. I've thought of starting French but we haven't enough space.'[16]

Nor were notions of deficiency and disadvantage restricted to immigrant languages. Their cultures, even when recognized as different, soon became stereotyped. West Indians were characterized as good at sport and music but unacademic and often unco-operative in class. Asians, on the other hand, were felt to be more passive and hardworking. Even so, their academic aspirations were felt to be unrealistic. Parents from both groups were assumed to be uninterested in their children's education, despite very strong indications to the contrary. Sadly, there is evidence that these stereotypes are still widespread today.[17]

Ethnic-minority children, like working-class children before them, were considered problems. Both groups received special attention from the Department of Education and Science's (DES) Education Disadvantage Unit which set up in the 1970s. There is little evidence of a change in official attitudes since that time. In 1981 the DES disregarded a recommendation from the Home Affairs Committee that a separate unit concerned solely with multi-racial education should be established to avoid any suggestion that ethnic-minority children were in some way deficient. The DES library still arranges books on multi-racial education alongside those on special education and disability.[18]

The Plowden Report

By the time Lady Plowden's Committee of Inquiry into Children and their Primary Schools began to take evidence in the mid-1960s, research indicated that closer links between home and schools were essential for educational advance. The committee drew on existing and specially commissioned research on the relationship between home and school and how this might affect the level of children's attainment. It concluded that differences in home background explained more of the variation in children's school achievements than did differences in educational provision and that it was therefore vitally important to involve parents more closely in the education of their children.

While the research on which the Plowden Report drew demonstrated without a doubt the differences in achievement between working- and middle-class children, the interpretation of these findings was sometimes woefully inadequate.[19] This can be illustrated by the way in which, for the purposes of statistical analysis, they clustered together variables as disparate as 'parent attendance at Open Evenings' and 'parental wish for children to receive post-compulsory education', under the heading of 'interest in education'. Researchers thus failed to realize that parents may not have attended Open Evenings because of difficulties over shift-work, or simply because they felt too intimidated, and that they may none the less have been very interested in their children's education.

There is now ample evidence to suggest that all parents – with a small number of pathological exceptions – are interested in the education of their children.[20] When given a specific task and adequate guidance and assurance, the majority of parents from all social and ethnic backgrounds have been found to be anxious to help their children. There is also evidence from outside mainstream education of a high level of parental interest. For instance, the setting up by the British Black community of Saturday or supplementary schools to teach skills which parents believe their children are not learning in mainstream schools seriously challenges the widespread stereotype of Black parents who do not care about their children's education.[21]

Ironically the main thrust for the Plowden Report was essentially the same as that of traditional educationalists: responsibility for the poor educational performance of working-class children was placed very firmly on the shoulders of working-class families themselves rather than on the school. School is seen as compensating for the deficiencies of home; working-class and ethnic-minority children are believed to be lacking in those essential skills which middle-class children acquire before they reach the school gates. Although the deficit model was challenged and discredited on many different fronts throughout the 1970s, many teachers still cling to the idea that their task is to compensate for disadvantage.

This position has come under increasing fire. It has been argued that suffering from socio-economic disadvantage is not at all like suffering from a vitamin deficiency: the solution is not as simple as dosing the patient with appropriate levels of compensation. It has also been suggested that labels such as 'disadvantage' and 'deprivation' are more a reflection of dominant class values than objective truth. Just because something is different, it does not necessarily follow that it is deficient.

With the value of hindsight, the preoccupation with class differences in education in the 1950s, 1960s, and much of the 1970s, seems very much like a smokescreen obscuring a vitally important issue. While the difference in the performance of middle-class and working-class children is indeed a question of serious concern for educators, the treatment which this matter received in the Plowden Report had the effect of diverting attention from the notion that *all* parents should have more access to and a greater say in the schooling of their children.

None the less, the Plowden Report was to be a watershed in the development of parental involvement in school. For the first time a government report set out a programme for contact between home and school. It recommended that the head and the class teacher should meet children before beginning school; that parents should meet with teachers and see children's work regularly; that teachers should visit homes; that primary schools should be used as much as possible out of school hours; and that parent-teacher associations should be formed. There was clearly an assumption that if schools were able to communicate to parents what they were trying to do, parental attitudes would become more favourable and, in due course, children's attitudes and achievements would improve.

For the first time there was an official acceptance of the importance of involving parents in their children's education and recommendations as to how this involvement should be achieved. Catchphrases such as 'parental involvement', 'parents as partners' and 'schools without walls' rapidly became assimilated into the vocabulary of educationalists. The basic premise that home-school links should be encouraged has been endorsed in a succession of publications, including government reports, which have appeared in the intervening years.[22] The publication of the report also stimulated a great deal of important discussion in the decade which followed on questions such as the accountability of schools and the purpose and quality of home-school relationships.

Chapter 3

Parents after Plowden

The Plowden Report (1967) placed home-school relations firmly on the agenda of many schools for the first time. The basic recommendations regarding parents were aimed at bridging the traditional distance between parents and teachers, whether through the formation of parent-teacher associations, or through initiatives for informing parents about the progress of their children and the working of the school. But to what extent were these recommendations actually implemented?

A survey carried out by Cyster and his colleagues in the late 1970s[1] seems to indicate that, by and large, the basic recommendations of Plowden were being implemented in most schools by this time. Almost all of the schools consulted held parents' evenings and open days which were generally well attended; it was also the norm that new parents were invited to visit before their children started school. Over half the headteachers said that parent attitudes had changed markedly since they had been allowed better access to the school and that they would welcome more parental involvement in a wider variety of activities.

However, while home-school relations were showing clear signs of improvement, it has to be acknowledged that progress in the decade following the Plowden Report was both slow and conservative and that much of the potential for teacher-parent collaboration remained untapped. The 1980 and 1986 Education Acts, however, have had the effect of renewing much of the debate of the late sixties and early seventies, strengthening and extending the rights of parents to be involved in their children's schooling.

In this chapter we will discuss the ways in which parental participation has developed in three important areas. The first of these areas is the work of parent-teacher associations which was first officially endorsed by Plowden. The second is the improvement of communications between home and school, first recommended by Plowden and given added weight by the 1980 and 1986 Education Acts. The third area is the right of parents to be represented on the governing bodies of schools, established by the 1980 Act and strengthened by the 1986 Act.

Parents as supporters

One of the recommendations of the Plowden Report was the formation of parent-teacher associations.[2] PTAs were seen as a promising means of involving parents in the life of the school. By allowing both sides of the educational partnership to meet socially as individuals rather than in their roles as parents and teachers, it was hoped that traditional barriers would be broken down. Many issues which parents felt unable to raise in the formal setting of the classroom or the headteacher's office could be broached more successfully in the informal surroundings of a social or fund-raising event.

PTAs serve a social function not only in encouraging good relations between parents and teachers but in cementing relationships between the parents themselves. They play a potentially important role, for instance, in disseminating information and welcoming new parents to the school. Most PTAs have a notice-board with announcements of social and fund-raising events and requests for help. Many school booklets contain information about the activities of the PTA. It is also quite common for members of the PTA to be available to talk to new parents on the first day of a new term. Activities of this kind have the advantage of being completely non-threatening to traditional assumptions of the teacher's role as 'expert'. For this reason PTAs were the area of school-home relations which made most rapid progress following Plowden.

However, PTAs were by no means a new development. The parent-teacher association is almost certainly the oldest form of voluntary organization supporting the school and dates back to well before the Plowden Report. A loose confederation of PTAs – the National Confederation of Parent-Teacher Associations

(NCPTA) – was formed in 1956, but isolated local organizations based on individual schools had been in existence for a number of years prior to this. PTAs have enjoyed a rather checkered history, starting from an uncertain base but gaining in momentum in the mid-1970s. Changing attitudes towards parental involvement in their children's schooling are faithfully mirrored in the changing fates of PTAs. Between 1975 and 1987 the National Confederation grew from 1,045 to 5,800 local associations. It thus represents some 5 million parents and nearly 200,000 teachers and is continuing to grow at around 10 per cent a year.

PTAs were not universally welcomed in the early days by headteachers and teachers. It was often argued that the time taken up by the administrative work involved in running a PTA could be better spent in other ways. There was also uncertainty about who should be in control of the PTA and whose ends should be served. The Plowden Report, for instance, expressed concern about PTAs falling into the control of a small caucus of determined parents. Many teachers felt, too, that if they met parents frequently on an informal basis there was simply no necessity for a formal organization.

Criticisms of PTAs have come from other quarters, too. A great many schools began by limiting the number of places available for elected representatives and constructing parent committees on the basis of one representative for a pre-determined number of families. Many people find the machinery of formal committees – motions, minutes and resolutions – is very off-putting and groups of this kind will only attract a certain kind of parent. This same machinery can also be used by the headteacher to control parents and deny them any real say in what is happening.

Fund-raising events

We have already discussed the social aspect of involvement in PTAs. Much of this social activity is, of course, based around fund-raising which is simultaneously the most common and most controversial aspect of the work of parent-teacher associations. Reports from Her Majesty's Inspectors of Schools in 1983 and 1984[3] confirmed what had already been known at a grass-roots level for several years, namely that schools were becoming increasingly dependent on home-school association funds. A survey undertaken by the National Confederation of Parent-Teacher Associations in 1985[4] shows quite clearly the extent of this dependence; 82 per cent of PTAs which responded reported that they had been asked by their schools to buy essentials. What precisely constitutes an 'essential' is, of course, problematic. The NCPTA worked on the assumption that if an item of equipment was provided in one school which could not be provided in another, then the pupils in the less well-equipped school would be disadvantaged and the item would therefore become 'essential' in their eyes. Using this definition, 'essentials' include textbooks, library books, micro-computing equipment, minibuses, furniture and school redecoration.

The increase in fund-raising activities and the changing patterns of spending of PTAs over the two years between 1981–2 and 1983–4 would suggest that parents are becoming increasingly aware of the problems which schools face. In 1981–2 spending was usually limited to audio-visual equipment and the occasional video-cassette recorder. In 1983–4 the bulk of spending was on micro-computers, giving a clear indication that parents consider the current level of computer education to be woefully inadequate and want to improve their children's access to 'hands–on' experience. In the same period, parental perception of the problems of providing adequate books has heightened as, too, has the desire to improve the environment in which their children work. There has been a four-fold increase in expenditure by PTAs on books and PTA spending on school buildings has more than doubled.

One of the unfortunate consequences of educational cutbacks is the creation of a two-tier state system of education in which many children will suffer through no fault of their own. Some schools, especially those in more affluent areas, will manage to raise large amounts of money to subsidize the education which their children are receiving. A good number of schools receive funding from parent organizations equivalent to their capitation allowance; a few actually receive more. Other schools where, for a variety of reasons, fund-raising efforts take place on a smaller scale, will inevitably find themselves at a disadvantage in terms of the educational opportunities they can offer their pupils.

It has also been argued that fund-raising activities absorb too much energy and detract from efforts to establish a true educational partnership between parents and teachers. What is more, too great an emphasis on fund-raising could potentially decrease membership of PTAs, because people dislike being continually asked to part with their own money or may be afraid of being dragged into persuading other people to part with theirs.

The PTA as a pressure group

In the present political climate the main function of the PTA will inevitably be to raise funds for the school. Yet there is a growing awareness of alternative roles for parent-teacher associations. The Scottish Parent Teacher Council (SPTC),[5] for instance, defines a PTA as 'a group of people who recognize that the education of a child is a process of partnership between parents and teachers, and who wish to take joint action to improve the quality of that partnership' (SPTC 1983).

One of the offshoots of increasing contact between parents and teachers is a growth in mutual understanding and respect. Parent delegates from a cross-section of Newcastle schools who attended a recent conference organized by the National Association for Primary Education reported educational priorities very similar to those frequently voiced by teachers.[6] These included smaller class sizes, lower teacher-pupil ratios and better resources to equip children with the technological skills they would need in the future. The potential of PTAs to act as pressure groups for increased educational spending is clearly considerable.

The Newcastle parents also rated parent-teacher collaboration as a priority. They wanted more school-based workshops for parents, and joint in-service courses to be run for teachers and parents. They felt that there should be open access to classrooms and more opportunity to express their views. Ideas such as these are being articulated by parent groups with growing frequency and strength.

Parents as consumers

Other basic recommendations of the Plowden Report concerned the importance of communicating information to parents about both individual children and the school's education philosophy and practice. These recommendations have subsequently been enacted as legal requirements under the terms of the 1980 and later the 1986 Education Acts. Local Education Authorities and schools must now furnish parents with information on school policy and organization. Various other developments in the 1980s have also strengthened the view of parents as the indirect consumers of education. The most notable of these are the right of parents to be represented on governing bodies; the development of a national curriculum which, among other things, will encourage parents to judge the achievements of schools; the question of greater parental choice of school; and the possibility of maintained schools opting out of local authority control.

It should be mentioned, however, that many people consider that developments of this kind are in the best interest of neither parents nor children. Uneasiness about the precise aims and wider implications of a national curriculum and testing of children at 7, 11, 14 and 16 has led certain parent groups to threaten civil disobedience.[7] Suggestions that schools should be able to opt out on the basis of a simple majority of parents have been attacked as unworkable and inviting chaos and resentment.[8] And the notion of parental choice of school has been criticized on the grounds that increasing choice for some will mean a denial of choice for others.[9]

The notion of accountability to parents as the indirect consumers of education has two distinct interpretations. The first concerns the expectation that schools should give an account of themselves to parents, informing them about policy matters and developments. This interpretation meets with widespread approval. The second, more controversial, interpretation is that schools are answerable to parents and must provide the kind of education which they demand. The dangers of the divide and rule mentality promoted by expectations of this kind are becoming increasingly clear: good relations built up between teachers and parents over many years are likely to be sorely tested. However, it is the first interpretation of accountability which forms the basis for the discussion which follows.

Communication between home and school

If teachers are to give an account of themselves to parents, good communication between school and home on all aspects of school life – from school policies and rules, to children's progress and the curriculum – is essential. This communication takes two main forms. First, there is the question of personal contact: what do parents do if they want to talk to the headteacher or class teacher? How are parents and children introduced to the school? How does the school report on individual children's progress? Second, how does the school handle written communication to the parents? Is the tone authoritative or informal? Is the style accessible?

Importance of style/tone of communication

Questions such as these are extremely important. Parents can feel welcome or held at bay; valued or dismissed. Their willingness and ability to become partners in their children's education is greatly influenced by the school's communicative style. Legislative requirements that the school keep parents informed do not in any way ensure that parents also feel welcome on the premises.

Making contact

The history of parent-teacher relations can be encapsulated in the signs displayed outside schools. In the early years of compulsory education, when parents were not encouraged to pass beyond the school gates, the signs read starkly, 'Parents must not step over this line'. Gradually parents were tolerated in the playground but not in the school building itself and the original notices gave way to the scarcely less hostile instruction: 'Please will parents not come into the corridors'. The growing awareness of the educative role of parents made their total exclusion from the school less acceptable, but there was still a feeling that they should enter the school only on the school's terms. This approach is characterized in the change to signs which read, 'Parents are welcome if they make appointments'. Increasingly, though, schools have started to display, 'Parents and visitors, you are welcome' signs, often translated into one or more languages.

Of course, responsibility for welcoming parents does not end with a sign outside the building. There are very great differences between schools in both their openness to outsiders and the ways in which they go about their daily routine. The messages communicated to parents and visitors by the physical environment of the school are very powerful. Do parents congregate outside or inside the school? Do they feel free to go into their children's classroom or are they uncomfortable about crossing the threshold? Are the headteacher and class teachers accessible or do parents have to make an appointment? Are teachers the only visible adults, or do parents, grandparents and other adults play a part in the life of the school? Does the visual environment of the school reflect traditional white middle-class values, or the multi-racial and multi-cultural composition of present-day Britain? These and many other questions need to be addressed by teachers who are serious in their intentions to involve parents in their children's schooling.

Letters home

One of the basic recommendations of the Plowden Report was that parents should be given more information about what was happening in schools. A great deal of this information is communicated to parents in writing, either in the form of school brochures or through letters sent home by 'pupil post'. The style, presentation and quality of these written communications can give important clues about the nature of relationships between schools and parents. Are they friendly and informative or do they use formal and off-putting language? And what about the content?

A group of practising teachers and researchers at Nottingham University[10] who examined a wide range of communications between home and school have distinguished four main kinds. The first is the 'Basic Information model', which sees the role of the parent in the educational process as limited and peripheral. This approach is summed up in the oft-quoted words of one headmaster: 'All I ask of parents is that they should bring it [*sic*] to school clean and well-dressed. I shall do the rest'.[11] Contents of such communications usually revolve around school hours, uniform, arrangements for meals and travel, school rules, school organization and homework.

The second kind of communication has been labelled the 'Public Relations model'. Its aim is to try and put across a positive image of the school and to enlist parental support. This model carefully selects aspects of school life, tailoring the selection to the projected needs, anxieties and wishes of parents. A great deal of attention is paid to layout, style and presentation.

The least common kind of communication, the 'Developmental model', addresses the question of children entering the school and suggests ways of making the transition as painless as possible. It typically includes information on entry or transfer arrangements, discussion of the differences between home and school, or primary and secondary schools, positive and constructive suggestions for parents and pupils, and, sometimes in the case of secondary schools, reassuring letters from last year's entrants.

Finally, we find the 'Parental Involvement model' which differs from the Basic Information model in both style and content. There is evidence of an open relationship with parents – 'When you come to see us, you will notice . . .' and specific mention is made of home-school relations. More emphasis is put on educational matters and suggestions are made as to how parents can help children to learn.

Written communication is not only reserved for matters concerning arrival or transfer to a school. Even the most mundane letters home, on subjects as diverse as school outings and head lice, can reveal a great deal about how the school views the role of parents. Parents are more likely to respond more warmly when they are made to feel as if they have an important – and equal – role in their children's education, than when they are issued with autocratic pronouncements on how and what they and their children should do.

Information on the curriculum

Another attempt to involve parents in their children's learning process has been through talks, exhibitions, discussions and workshop activities which centre on the different curriculum areas which are taught in the school. Videos are also sometimes used for supporting activities in this area. In one teacher-training experiment sponsored by the Community Development Education Centre, for instance, student teachers are videoed working in the classroom and are then asked to explain to parents what they are doing. A number of other videos are also available in English and several Asian languages on various aspects of the curriculum and the way in which parents can become involved in the life of the school.[12]

The way in which the school presents information on the curriculum is extremely important. Informal meetings would appear to work much better than formal talks where discussions and questioning are mediated by the headteacher. Parental involvement in deciding both the format of meetings and which areas need to be covered would also seem to be a prerequisite for success. When such events work well they can be extremely valuable for all concerned. Parents who understand what teachers are trying to do, and why, are likely to be far more supportive than those whose lack of information leaves them feeling anxious and confused.

Parent pressure

The need for schools to communicate with parents was raised, of course, by the Plowden Report (1967) and was reinforced by the 1980 Education Act. A more novel aspect of recent legislation, however, is the requirement that parents should be represented on the governing bodies of schools. Much of the pressure for representation of this kind has come from the various parent groups which have arisen over the last three decades and which have slowly but surely made a serious impression on policy and practice.

This growth needs to be seen within a broader context. The 1960s saw a mushrooming of client and consumer and minority interest groups: the Consumer Association, the National Association of Managers and Governors, Shelter, the Child Poverty Action Group and the Patients' Association, to name just a few. Interestingly, parent groups did not achieve much prominence in this period. Although some schools had voluntarily included parents on their governing bodies during the 1970s, parental rights to representation were only established in law in the 1980 Education Act. The reorganization of education along comprehensive lines had been the major preoccupation of the 1970s and parents' rights as consumers failed to appear on the educational agenda.

PTAs were the first school-based organizations. They were followed in the 1960s by a number of alternative groupings. The most important of these were the Associations for the Advancement of State Education (AASE), which cover the area of the local education authority (LEA) and are linked nationally through the Campaign for the Advancement of State Education (CASE). Like the NCPTA, CASE has grown considerably in recent years, increasing the number of local groups by 12 between 1986 and 1987 to reach a national total of 47.

There has also been a burgeoning of local groups set up to address local issues. The Association of Sheffield Parents, for instance, has spearheaded the campaign against tertiary colleges in the city, while the Hackney Association for Kids' Education has been pressing for accommodation for teachers experiencing difficulty because of housing shortages and high property prices. In this way, they hope to attract new staff to fill existing vacancies.

Groups such as these often attract criticism on the grounds that their members are not representative of parents as a whole: they attract middle-class people who are not intimidated by formal organizations. Whatever the validity of this view, parent groups have contributed to many important changes in the ways in which schools are run, not least of which is the right of parents to better information and to representation on the board of governors.

The 1977 Taylor Report[13] first recommended that parents should be appointed governors in primary schools in response to the considerable demand for greater accountability articulated by many parent groups. This recommendation was taken up by the government and included in the 1980 Education Act. Under the terms of the Act, parents elected by a secret ballot of all parents in the school should act as representatives on governing bodies of all maintained schools in England and Wales. It was argued that this move would make schools more responsive and accountable to the neighbourhoods which they served.

It should also be pointed out that this development has been seen by some observers as having a distinctly political motivation.[14] It has been widely assumed that parents are a force for conservatism: the majority want old-fashioned results and are suspicious of educational experiments and innovation. The inclusion of parents on boards of governors can therefore be construed as an attempt to ensure that demands for a traditional curriculum will prevail. Parents are seen as powerful allies in what has often been presented as the fight against classroom extremists.

Ironically, this view would seem to have little substance. During the protracted teacher dispute which started in 1985, for instance, Kenneth Baker as Education Secretary repeatedly claimed parental support for his decision to impose a settlement on, and remove the bargaining rights from, teachers' unions. Yet the major parent pressure groups, while condemning the continuing disruption in schools, did not waver in their support of the teachers' claims for better educational provision.[15] It seems probable that parent governors will be concerned as much with issues such as government spending policies and class sizes as with radical local education policies.

Ideas first put forward in the 1980 Education Act were subsequently developed in various government papers and were finally incorporated into the 1986 Education Act. For instance, parent representation has been greatly increased leading to an estimated 20,000 more parent governors nationwide. Yet, while the notion of parent representation is applauded by all sides of the political spectrum, its implementation raises a whole range of intractable problems and, for this reason, the 1986 Act is currently attracting a great deal of criticism.

The election of parent governors

The 1986 Education Act decrees that parent representatives should be fairly and democratically elected by secret ballot. Various individuals and groups, most notably the National Association of Governors and Managers (NAGM), have pointed out that, as things stand at the moment, this aim is more complex than one might at first expect. All too often, nominations for parent governors do not exceed the number of places available and there is no contest, leaving headteachers open to the criticism that parents become governors through selection rather than election. In order to ensure that the person elected is truly representative of the parent body as a whole, it has been argued that schools should hold hustings where candidates can say something about themselves, their interests and concerns. Yet in one case, the local authority has limited the manifesto to thirty-six words; and in others, candidates have only been able to reach other parents by handing out duplicated sheets at home time.[16]

Reporting back

Once elected, an essential part of the parent governors' role is the reporting back to fellow parents after governors' meetings. However, this often proves to be extremely difficult. Where parent governors make use of the school machinery and send duplicated letters there have been complaints that these often have to receive the headteacher's seal of approval. There have even been instances of schools and authorities refusing point blank to co-operate with parent governors' attempts to disseminate information. For instance, Devon's Chief Education Officer sent a letter in 1984 forbidding parent governors from contacting other parents 'through the school machinery . . . or by letters taken home by children'.[17] The notion of representativeness becomes a mockery when parent governors are expected to work under conditions such as these.

Governing bodies as a whole, however, have new responsibilities under the 1986 Education Act and are now legally bound to report back to the parent body at a formally convened annual meeting. The first of these meetings was arranged rather hurriedly towards the end of the summer term 1987 in compliance with the terms of the Act. Governing bodies were required to prepare and circulate a written report to parents in advance of the meeting. Some concern has been expressed about whether governing bodies contain enough people capable of compiling documents of this kind and there is a general suspicion that most reports were prepared by the headteacher with a little help from the chairperson of the governors. Many people also fear that the extra demands placed on governors by these requirements will deter many parents from standing for election to the governing body.[18]

The purpose of these meetings is to make the governing bodies more accountable to parents and to allow parents to express both support and reservations. When the meetings are quorate – with 20 per cent of parents in attendance – they have the power to pass resolutions. Teacher unions expressed serious reservations about the meetings, fearing attacks from parents on individual teachers, and advised their members not to attend. In the event, however, many teachers did attend the meetings and the unions' fears appeared to have been unfounded.

The picture which has emerged from these first parent-governor meetings is a rather embarrassing one. Low attendances have been reported nationwide and schools which achieved a quorum were very rare indeed. In many primary schools the number of parents attending was in single figures, while very few secondary schools achieved treble figures. Most parents seem to find the idea of formal meetings of this kind unattractive. This raises some important issues. It is possible, for instance, that meetings will be used by individual parents, or small parent groups, as a platform to air their grievances. Decisions which may be taken thus risk being unrepresentative of the views of the parent body as a whole.

Representativeness of parent governors

The same criticism which has been levied against parent pressure groups can also be made against parent governors. The majority of parent representatives are middle class, and the proportion of women and ethnic-minority governors is much lower than it should be.[19] A major factor in perpetuating this state of affairs is the lack of information offered to parents. An obvious consequence is that most parents are often only vaguely aware of the existence of governors, let alone their precise functions, and are therefore unlikely to offer themselves for election. The new demands being made on governing bodies to prepare annual reports and make a public defence of their actions are also likely to have the effect of deterring all but the most articulate and confident of parents.

There are practical considerations, too. Primary schools are, of course, neighbourhood schools, but many children are involved in a good deal of travel at the secondary stage. When this is the case, the financial burden of attendance at meetings can be heavy for the lower paid and the unemployed, yet travelling expenses are discretionary. Nor has enough attention been paid to covering the costs of arranging for the care of children or the elderly in the case of single parents or other carers.

Training

Many parents find themselves in a very uncomfortable position when they first become governors, especially if they have little previous committee experience or knowledge of how the education system works.[20] They may be confronted with well-organized political appointees who have a clearly defined agenda; with headteachers whose tactics are sometimes to stonewall any attempts at influencing what takes place in the school; and with local community figures who often see their job as simply one of supporting the headteacher. A parent governor unversed in the etiquette and procedures of committee work can be no match for more experienced and sometimes hostile colleagues.

There have been reports in the press that parent governors'

views are welcome on more mundane matters to do with the everyday running of the school, such as locks on lavatory doors, but are effectively excluded from staff selection and appointment panels. Parents have also complained about feeling embarrassed and patronized when they have raised questions perceived by more experienced colleagues as naive or inappropriate.[21] If parent governors are to play a full and equal role in the governing of schools it is therefore essential that they should be offered some kind of training.

Yet opportunities for training range, with a few notable exceptions, from inadequate to non-existent. Only half of the local authorities in England and Wales have offered any governor training. Most of this was in the wake of the Taylor Report (1977) and was short-lived. In contrast, the demand for training is considerable. When the NAGM began their own regional training programme in 1985 they found that their courses were massively oversubscribed. In view of the large number of schools to be covered and the turnover of parent governors every two to three years, efforts such as this can do little more than scratch the surface.

Parents with power?

The recent legislation leaves many questions unanswered. While few people doubt the need for the schools to inform parents either of their children's progress or of what is happening in the school, developments in the appointment of parent governors are more controversial. To what extent does it offer parents real power? How representative of the parent body as a whole are individual governors? Is it often the case that parent governors are denied a full and equal role because of their lack of training, or because they feel intimidated by other governors who see their main function as supporting the *status quo*? Even if no clear or satisfactory answers for questions such as these are forthcoming at the present, we can confidently predict that the next decade will be a very interesting one.

In short

The involvement of parents in many aspects of their children's schooling, first advocated by the Plowden Report (1967), has developed slowly over the past twenty years. Early attempts to make schools more accessible to parents were aimed at producing more favourable attitudes towards education in working-class families which would ultimately improve the performance of their children. The changing mood of the intervening years has gradually reshaped the character and the intentions of parental involvement: there is now a widespread recognition of the need for schools to be accountable to all parents for the education which is being offered to their children.

It is common practice now for schools to welcome parents in the role of supporters through the various parent-teacher association activities. Parents are represented on governing bodies and schools are aware of their responsibility to involve them in their children's schooling by informing them both of their child's progress and of the school's philosophy and practice. In some cases, this is an obligation imposed by law; in others it is a responsibility which schools have undertaken willingly and with a great deal of thought and effort – in an attempt to develop a meaningful relationship with parents. Yet it is possible to involve parents in all these spheres of activity without their crossing the threshold of the school more than once or twice a year when they attend an open day, a parents' evening, a governors' meeting or an event organized by the PTA. The question remains as to whether this is the only level of parent participation which is desirable, or whether parents seek a more active involvement in their children's schooling.

Chapter 4

Parents in school

The message from Plowden onwards was clear: parents needed to be persuaded of the value of the school's work and this would best be achieved by involving them in the life of the school. The nature of that involvement, however, was limited. Parents could be encouraged, for instance, to help in fund-raising or improving the school environment. Yet more centrally educational questions were still seen to be the territory of teachers. Similarly, the emphasis of the 1980 and 1986 Education Acts is on the parent as the indirect consumer of education, rather than as a more active participant in the everyday life of the school.

In the early days of parental involvement, teacher-parent relations could reasonably be described as superficial; and it was teachers rather than parents who determined the terms of the relationship. The move from this position was slow. By the late seventies, however, many teachers were beginning to take the parents' role in their children's education more seriously and were making important strides towards involving them more meaning-fully in the life of the school. Reports of more active parental involvement in school started to surface.[1]

In this chapter we will look at how the involvement of parents in the daily life of schools has developed. Early initiatives drew on parent helpers for a small number of specific educational tasks. Gradually parents have become more centrally involved in areas of the curriculum which have been the traditional preserve of teachers. The benefits reported by all parties – parents, children and teachers – suggest that a reappraisal of the parent-teacher relationship is long overdue. Is it possible to foster a genuine partnership between the two main forces in children's education and, if so, how can this be achieved?

Parents as helpers

The nature of parental involvement at this level has been varied. In some cases, parents work alongside the class teacher very much in the role of unpaid teachers' aides, performing tasks such as tidying the library and repairing books, taking children swimming or accompanying them on outings. In other cases, parents are allowed more initiative, and offer help in areas outside the core curriculum, such as recorder class, sewing, cooking and pottery.

In some schools an invitation is offered to all parents to help in the classroom either in the school booklet or through letters sent home with children. However, many schools are highly selective about who performs this role, with teachers showing a marked preference for parents who share their own background and values. It would seem that the majority of parents invited into the classroom are white, middle class and educated. There are also reports that there is a clear division between the kind of help offered by middle-class and working-class parents: working-class parents usually offer servicing help, whereas middle-class parents tend to offer a skill such as art, pottery or music.

Some schools have realized the educational potential of the wider community, and draw regularly on the expertise of parents, grandparents and community leaders. Sometimes they will be called upon to talk to children about some aspect of their own experience which is relevant to the work the children are doing or to demonstrate a particular skill. In many multi-racial schools, parents are invited to tell stories in their mother tongues and to act as translators and interpreters. A recurring feature of all of these initiatives, however, is that there are very clear lines of demarcation between the teacher and the parent, and basic subjects remain, by and large, the territory of the teacher.

Pros and cons of parents in school

The growth of parental involvement in school has encountered some vociferous opposition. Parental involvement has often been seen as making the teacher's job even more difficult: it takes time, creates stress and demands more staff. This view was forcefully put forward, for instance, at the 1969 Conference of Headteachers where a resolution was passed stressing that parental participation, if carried to extremes, could operate to the disadvantage of children. In an address from the floor, heads were told that parental involvement could end up being a Frankenstein monster which had run out of control.

Yet it is possible to use arguments similar to those offered by the headteachers to make a counter-case. Parents provide help for the hard-pressed class teacher; they make it possible for children to take part in a wider range of activities than would otherwise be possible and extend the range of one-to-one relationships with an adult in a classroom setting. Possible criticisms that parent helpers are merely compensating for shortages created by LEA financial cutbacks can be countered by the benefits accrued by parents: a better understanding and appreciation of what schools are trying to achieve and greater confidence about the role which they play in their children's learning.

The teacher as the 'expert'

The question of teacher expertise is critical in understanding the opposition to parental involvement which is still to be found in many quarters. Sensitivity about the expert status of teachers has a long history.[2] Teacher education took place for many years in an atmosphere of social and intellectual inferiority. Teachers were very often non-graduates and received a training far shorter than that of many other of the so-called professions. As a result, teachers occupied an ambiguous position: on the one hand, they acted as the guardians of society and prevailing social values; on the other hand, they themselves were denied access to the higher rungs of the social ladder. A National Union of Teachers (NUT) survey on the public's opinion of teachers carried out in 1969 showed that most people viewed teaching as a career which depended more on personality characteristics such as tolerance, patience and friendliness than on a high level of skill acquired through a long and difficult training.

Today the position is very different in that all new teachers have at least four years' education at degree level or beyond. Teacher awareness of the relationship between their training and their performance in the classroom is greater than ever before and it is not at all surprising that the question of teacher expertise should feature prominently on the agenda of both teaching unions and individual headteachers and teachers.

The Bullock Report (1976) encapsulated many teacher anxieties when it warned about 'misguided teaching from over-anxious parents' and parents 'whose efforts have been unsuccessful or positively harmful'. The NUT Report, *Home-School Relations and Adults in the School*,[3] expresses similar views on the importance of teacher expertise:

> The teacher's judgements are based on experience of other children and age groups, as well as on professional training. They are focused on a particular child by the teacher's knowledge of that child's work and attitudes, refined as a result of discussions with colleagues including the head, advisory staff, and the child's parents. No adult other than the teaching staff will possess that vital amalgam of knowledge, nor the responsibility of holding it in confidence. Professional responsibility consists in exercising this knowledge; the task cannot be delegated.
>
> (NUT 1983)

Parents and home reading schemes

While very few people would wish to challenge the premises on which this view is based, there are some who would question how precisely this policy position should be interpreted in practice. The case of parents and reading provides an excellent example of the philosophical and practical issues raised by the involvement of parents in school. The practice of schools enlisting the help of parents to listen to children reading has become increasingly common over the last ten years.[4] It has given rise to a number of interesting and highly innovative examples of teacher-parent collaboration. And yet it remains one of the most hotly contested issues in education.

For many teachers reading remains a sacrosanct area over which they want to retain complete control. Even in schools with a tradition of parent helpers, reading is sometimes felt to be the responsibility of teachers alone. On occasion, this view is so strongly held that teachers refuse to allow children to take school 'reading books' home. Anxieties are expressed about the harm which can be done by parents who do not understand the reading process: children might end up reading parrot fashion; they might be confused by different teaching methods; or they might feel too pressured.

In spite of these deeply held objections, many other teachers have felt it essential to involve parents in the teaching of reading. One of the most significant developments in recent years has been the various home reading schemes in which parents are asked to hear their children read regularly. Most schemes depend on the use of report cards used for comments on the child's progress and other messages which allow the teacher to monitor progress and provide for good communication between home and school.

Home reading schemes were pioneered in Haringey, Belfield and Hackney and have subsequently spread to large numbers of schools in many different parts of the country. One of the interesting features of the original experiments was that they took place in urban schools, many of which had a high proportion of ethnic-minority and working-class parents. Support for the projects proved to be high and has helped to put paid to the myth that only middle-class parents are interested in – and capable of – helping with their children's learning. But possibly the most important reason that home reading schemes have attracted so much attention is the claim that they have significantly improved children's reading performance.

The question of what precisely is achieved by home involvement in reading is a complex one.[5] Increasingly, the adequacy of scores on standardized reading tests, the conventional measures of reading success, is coming under fire, and the gains in reading performance in the projects which have used these measures have been highly variable. What remains undisputed, however, is the mutual benefits to parents and children through parental involvement of this kind. Evaluations of home reading projects have consistently shown improvements in areas such as children's attitudes to books and reading; the relationships between parents and teachers; and parental self-confidence.

In terms of the overall gains achieved by home reading schemes of this kind, there would seem to be little support for teacher anxiety over parental involvement in the area of reading. But does the same hold true when we look more closely at what takes place? A Sheffield-based study undertaken by Hannon, Jackson & Page[6] set out to answer this question by analysing recordings of children reading to both parents and teachers. The parents, who all came from working-class families, were given no special training but received support and encouragement through meetings, some home visiting, home-school communication through reading cards and a general advice sheet. The parents' strategies were compared with those of the teachers in two areas generally held to be extremely important in the teaching of reading; miscues (when the child does not read a word accurately) and concern for understanding.

The researchers found that parents and teachers faced with a child who hesitates or reads a word incorrectly tend to respond in much the same way. They also established that both teachers and parents showed a concern for understanding, albeit in slightly different ways. Both groups of adults paid particular attention to understanding when the child was experiencing difficulty, whereas the teacher also showed concern at other points in reading. Overall, then, there was no evidence to support the idea that parents of so-called 'disadvantaged' children are inadequate in hearing their children read.

There is also a sense in which parents have made their own decisions about involving themselves in their children's learning. A rapid survey of most publishers' catalogues or the shelves of high street bookshops and newsagents reveals an amazing array of materials aimed at parents wishing to help their children at home. Indeed, several recently published school reading programmes make explicit reference in their teachers' notes to parental involvement.[7]

Parents and reading in school

Our picture of the role which parents play in reading in a school setting is based largely on a research project directed by Barry Steirer between 1983 and 1985.[8] It took the form of a postal survey of practice in nearly 400 primary schools, followed up with in-depth interviews in a sub-sample of thirty of the schools who took part in the original survey. Over half these schools were asking volunteers to help in school on a regular basis. Actual practice varied a great deal in the numbers of helpers; how they were approached; which children they worked with; and how they went about it. But, in most cases, parents listened to the more fluent readers on a one-to-one basis under the supervision of the class teacher.

It is ironic that schools who used parent helpers for hearing children read justified this practice in terms very similar to those who were not prepared to countenance it. Those against parental involvement stressed that learning to read requires the professional support of a trained teacher; those who used parent helpers argued that reading was too important an activity to be left solely to the hard-pressed class teacher. Some schools felt that because many of their parents have literacy problems of their own, experience difficult domestic circumstances or speak little English, it was inappropriate to involve them in reading with their children. Other schools stress that reading is a very effective way of involving all parents in their children's learning. Some schools said that it would be harmful to invite parents because they had a large number of children with reading problems. Others had decided to involve parents precisely because reading problems were so prevalent.

In schools where parents regularly heard children reading two main benefits were identified. The first related directly to children's reading: headteachers talked of improved reading performance, extra practice, greater interest in reading and the usefulness of being able to talk to an adult about reading. The second benefit was more indirect: it included the parent's growth in understanding of the reading process and books in general; a better appreciation of what the school was trying to achieve; and the opportunity for children to have a one-to-one relationship with an adult other than the teacher in the classroom. The only area in which doubts were raised as to the validity of the practice was whether parent-helpers were being used to compensate for staff shortages imposed by LEA cut-backs in finance.

Parents for their part felt that they were helping their own children – even though they often worked with other children – by gaining a better understanding of what was involved in the reading process. Many parents had volunteered their services because of direct pressure from their own child and they found it interesting to see him or her relating to other children in a school setting. They showed interest in the children that they worked with and enthusiasm at the progress which they made over a period of time. They also expressed their appreciation of class teachers and admiration for their patience, resourcefulness and good humour.

Parents and other areas of the curriculum

When parents are allowed to work with their own or other children on what is ususally defined as 'the core curriculum', the first focus is invariably reading. Gradually, however, there are signs of parents being allowed to work in other areas previously considered the exclusive domain of teachers. One such example is the parents' writing project which started in Thomas Buxton School in Spitalfields, London, in 1979.[9] A high proportion of the children in this inner-city school came from bilingual backgrounds. In an attempt to involve parents more closely in the work of the school and to acknowledge the linguistic diversity in their midst, two teachers approached parents about the possibility of working together to write books in the mother tongue. The reception was enthusiastic. Stories were usually based on the child, the family or childhood memories. First drafts were tried out on the children in the classroom and teachers and parents would then edit the writing before typing up the final version and adding the illustrations.

The project was not, of course, confined to bilingual families, and also drew on English-speaking parents. But if a book was written in a language other than English, a second copy was produced in translation. Some of the books produced in this way were quite widely distributed with copies being given not only to the classroom and the school library but to the local teachers' centre and the wider community. The idea spread from Spitalfields first to other schools in Lambeth and then well beyond, and promises to be as attractive an initiative as many of the home reading schemes.

Another project which extended the bounds of parent involvement in the core curriculum was started in 1981 in Foxhill Primary School in Sheffield.[10] Parents were asked to work in school with their own children. A single group made up of 5–6 year-old children from three separate classes came together with their mothers and a teacher for an hour a week. Although reading was the main focus, mothers did not simply hear their children read. They were also involved, for instance, in playing language games and doing worksheets, with the teacher at hand to give advice and encouragement as it was needed. At the end of the first twelve months of this scheme, the parents who took part were so pleased that it was extended to all the first-year infant children and eventually to other areas of the curriculum.

IMPACT: parental involvement in maths

While parental involvement in reading and, to some extent, other language related areas, has become widely accepted, a great deal more controversy surrounds the role of parents in mathematics education. Until quite recently, the only home involvement in this area has been attendance at parents' evenings where teachers explain and defend the notion of 'modern maths'. However, IMPACT (Mathematics, Parents, Children and Teachers)[11] heralds important changes in yet another area which has previously been considered an exclusively teacher domain.

IMPACT was launched as an Inner London Education Authority (ILEA) pilot project in 1985–7 and was then taken further in a three year programme of research and development in a network of local education authorities, rural and urban. The scheme entails an initial meeting with parents; a well-prepared but flexible plan of work for the term; and a mathematical game or investigation which children take home each week to tackle with their parents.

The popularity of IMPACT with children, parents and teachers alike closely parallels reactions to home reading schemes. The one-to-one relationship allows for a range of detailed work which would be impossible in a normal classroom situation and both parents and teachers have reported that children show greatly increased enthusiasm for mathematical activities. Many parents have come to realize that you do not necessarily have to be good at something yourself to be able to help: they have become involved in the learning process and confidence, interest, and understanding between parents, teachers, children and their maths have grown.[12]

It has to be acknowledged that parental involvement in mathematics sometimes raises uncomfortable questions for teachers. Most notable is the concern generated by the blurring of the boundaries between teacher and parent which we have already discussed in relation to parents and reading. However, there are also issues which are peculiar to mathematics. The traditional hierarchy associated with learning in maths is often broken down. For instance, teachers are adamant that very young children do not deal with large numbers because they will not understand them; or that infants should not do 'scale' because it is too complicated a concept. Parents, however, assume that if children can do something, particularly if they can do it in a variety of situations, then they understand it. While this difference in approach between teachers and parents does not necessarily imply that we should return to rote learning and more traditional teaching techniques, it does seriously challenge our ideas of what counts as understanding in maths and the notion that there is only one 'right', way to teach a concept.

Parents as partners

The deficit model of education which underpinned both the Plowden (1967) and Bullock (1976) Reports and much of the educational practice which followed in their wake saw working-class and ethnic-minority children as 'disadvantaged'. Because teachers felt that the families of disadvantaged children were responsible for their educational underperformance, they tended to treat parents as clients rather than partners. Sheila Wolfendale, who has written extensively on this subject,[13] has pointed out that in a client relationship, parents are seen as dependent on experts' opinions; they are passive in the receipt of service; they are apparently in need of redirection; they are peripheral in decision-making; and they are felt to be 'inadequate' or 'deficient'.

The partnership in 'more than name' which was advocated by Plowden had little hope of success while negative attitudes towards parents remained unchallenged. Yet, while various government reports fostered the notion of parents as clients, much of the debate which they stimulated centred on the purpose and quality of home-school relations and helped to develop an alternative view of the role of parents in education: parents as partners.

Very few people today would argue with the notion that co-operation between parents and teachers is a good thing. Yet attempts to translate theory into practice vary from school to school, both in the degree of commitment shown by the teaching staff and in the different approaches which are used. Some schools have travelled a long way along the road to partnership with parents, but many cling resolutely to their traditional role as 'professionals'. We are forced to conclude that terms such as 'parent participation', 'parent involvement' or 'parent-teacher partnership' mean many different things to many different people.

While parent involvement in the curriculum has without a doubt been one of the most important developments in education in recent times, this model of parent participation is currently coming under attack from a number of directions. We have already examined the objections of some teachers and teacher unions concerned to protect their role as 'experts'. But there is also criticism from those who feel that parental involvement in the curriculum is just one aspect of home-school relationships, and a real and lasting partnership between parents and teachers will demand further changes of a much more radical nature.

Putting parents in the picture

The heir apparent to the curriculum-centred model of parent involvement is one which includes parents more centrally in the decision-making process.[14] Exponents of this approach point out that parents' knowledge of their own child is far greater than the teacher's. A logical extension of this argument is that the teacher's specialist knowledge about children and learning in general should complement the specific knowledge of parents. Most important, it is possible to argue further that, since both parents' and teachers' contributions to children's education are essential for learning to take place, they should be accorded equal status.

The move to a model of education which accords greater status to the parent does not necessarily entail introducing a whole new range of parent activities into the classroom. The difference lies rather in teacher attitudes and approaches. Wolfendale,[15] for instance, argues that the cardinal principle of reciprocity must operate if parents and teachers are to achieve a real and lasting partnership: mutual involvement, mutual accountability, mutual gain, and mutual trust. This model of partnership may at present seem nothing short of utopian for the majority of schools. Yet there is much to commend this approach for all parties concerned and evidence of moves in this direction in many schools.

It is also important to clarify that the equal partnership between parents and teachers is a status rather than a management issue. Teachers have traditionally been viewed as the senior partners who invariably know what is best for the child. Increasingly, however, parents are felt to bring a different and no less important perspective to their children's education. This partnership of equals does not, of course, apply to classroom management. The teacher inevitably takes overall responsibility for what happens in the classroom.

The teacher as facilitator

The use of parent help in core areas of the curriculum, as we have seen, posed a serious challenge to the traditional role of the teacher as the 'expert' who decides what should be taught and how. Those who advocate the still more radical move towards a genuine partnership with parents may be perceived as an even more serious threat to the *status quo*. Yet the pressure for change in this sphere has come from many different quarters, not least the recent revolution in information technology.[16] We live in a world where information systems are rapidly expanding and, according to some estimates, the quantity of knowledge is doubling every ten years. The traditional role of the teacher as the specialist transmitter of information is becoming untenable.

Our changed perception of the learning process also has implications for partnership with parents. There is a growing appreciation of the child as an active learner: adults create an atmosphere which facilitates learning rather than 'teaching'. Given this understanding, it is only reasonable that there should be some devolution of responsibility for activities previously considered to be the domain of teachers on to parents and community. Yet, such developments, far from deprofessionalizing teachers, call for a reprofessionalization along rather different lines. The most obvious scenario is to develop the school as a resource centre where the teacher is the chief organizer of learning resources, including the invaluable resources of parents and community.[17]

Educating the educators

Any move towards a genuine partnership with parents will create a demand for training on the part of both parents and teachers. There is already a well-established demand for courses for parent governors, but there are also indications that parents wish to learn more about both school organization and the curriculum. Many schools provide this kind of information in the form of talks on the curriculum and various workshop activities. The Community Development Education Centre (CDEC) is currently involved in development work with existing parents' and parent-teacher associations, and is also exploring new forms of parent groupings. This will involve training courses for parents who wish to involve themselves in their children's schooling, as well as those who are school governors.

There is also the question of teacher education. In initial teacher training, home/school relations need to be addressed as an important issue in all aspects of the curriculum rather than being treated as an optional or marginal concern. There are few signs, however, that this is the case. A 1985 report prepared by Atkin & Bastiani on *Preparing Teachers to Work with Parents*[18] showed that very little attention is currently being paid by colleges of higher education and universities to this subject at an initial training level.

The situation is scarcely any different for practising teachers. Various colleges of education, LEAs, as well as individual schools and organizations, are recognizing the importance of this question by putting on conferences and short training courses. However, there is also a need for longer INSET (In-Service Education for Teachers) provision and regular support sessions. The fact remains that teachers are not automatically good at relating to other adults: they need help to realize the potential of parents as equal partners and to develop the necessary skills for working with them.

Questions to answer

Over the last twenty or so years two quite distinct but complementary views on parental involvement in education have evolved. One of these views sees parents as consumers who should be given the opportunity to select their children's schools, be represented

who were/are experts
here draw line if one at all, some's up

on the governing bodies of schools and have a say in school policy.
The other sees parents as a resource: they play a central part in
the education of their children and it is important to exploit this
relationship by involving parents in the life of the school. Interestingly, the relation between the two movements – parents as
consumers and parents as a resource – is a very superficial one
inasmuch as the one could potentially have evolved quite independently of the other.

Yet there is an inevitable interaction between these points of
view. The notion of parents as a resource can be promoted in a
number of quite different ways. It is possible, for instance, for
teachers to view both parents and children as empty vessels
waiting to be filled with knowledge. Or it is possible to look on
parents as equal partners with complementary skills and knowledge. The move towards the notion of parents as equal partners
has almost certainly been fuelled by the development of the
parents' consumer movement.

Partnership with parents is a very challenging concept. It leads
us to ask new questions and the answers are not always apparent.
Up to the present many teachers' energies have focused on ways
of encouraging parents to become involved with their children's
schooling. More recent trends, in contrast, may make it necessary
to turn this issue on its head and ask instead whether there are
any specific teaching activities that parents should be excluded
from. Is it reasonable to allow some parents, because of their
special expertise, to work in some areas, but not others? Is there
some work you would undertake with your own children but not
with others?

The idea of a negotiated curriculum in which student and
teacher jointly determine what is to be studied has gained a great
deal of ground in recent years in higher education. It remains to
be seen, however, what will happen if this approach is applied in
a school setting. Many observers might feel that a curriculum
negotiated between parents, teachers and children would be
totally impractical because of the different and sometimes
conflicting views of those concerned. Yet such a view underesti-
mates the common ground held by teachers and parents and their
shared aspirations for children's education. The participation of
parents in this aspect of school life may well turn out to be no
less practical than their involvement in the teaching of reading

and other areas of school life. Nor will it in any way undermine the teacher's overall responsibility for classroom management and curriculum development.

It is possible to legislate for some aspects of change such as the requirement for schools to provide parents with information, or to allow them to be represented on governing bodies. It is not, however, possible to legislate for attitude change. The ways in which schools comply with the law reveal a great deal about teachers' attitudes towards parents. We are clearly dealing with a process in which some schools and teachers are considerably more advanced in their thinking than others.

The rate of change is a matter of speculation, though the recent teacher dispute and low teacher morale can only have the effect of seriously slowing it down. But the general direction of the change which is in progress is unmistakable. As they seek to redefine their own role, teachers are gradually working towards a genuine partnership with parents.

Part Two

Parents and school – from theory into practice

Chapter 5

Apprenticeship in the seventies

This part of the book is largely one teacher's view of how one particular school responded to the idea of parent participation in primary education. Parents' and children's comments complete the picture which spans seven years in the life of Redlands Primary School, Reading, from January 1980 to September 1987.

However, before joining the staff of Redlands, I taught for eight years at E.P. Collier, another Reading primary school which had a great deal in common with Redlands. It, too, was a medium-sized urban primary school serving a linguistically and culturally diverse community. It, too, saw the appointment of a new head-teacher committed to change, with parental involvement high on his list of priorities. It was at E.P. Collier that I served my apprenticeship as a primary school teacher and, because it was there that the foundations were laid for the process of parental involvement at Redlands, it is the logical place for me to start.

E.P. Collier: creating a team

I was appointed to E.P Collier in 1971 as a part-time French teacher. With the arrival of John Shearman, a young, first-time head shortly afterwards, it became obvious that the writing was on the wall as far as French was concerned. He clearly felt it to be a luxury in a school where English was already a second language for many of the children. I moved sideways to become a part-time teacher of English as a second language (E2L) at the same school. In that role, I was working alongside class teachers, becoming increasingly fascinated by seeing children of this age learn and develop, increasingly caught up in the educational theories and practice of the day. Two terms later, when a vacancy arose, I became a full-time primary class teacher. That is when the fun started! Having been thrown in at the deep end, I had an enormous amount of reading to catch up on, a lot of courses to attend, and hours of discussions with interested colleagues to engage in.

In the early seventies, I think everyone at that school, if asked, would have felt quite happy about relationships with parents. The school hosted the usual run of social events such as fairs and jumble sales. Parents' evenings were an established event, although the numbers attending were not impressive. The PTA committee was a small band of elected parents and teachers who got on with the business in hand which, at that point, was mainly fund-raising.

So, what did the new head offer? Firstly, a passionate belief in equality of education for all, regardless of creed, gender or race. Secondly, he was convinced, largely by Eric Midwinter's work in Liverpool,[1] about the role of the community in education: he intended to do his best to link home and school, those two major influences in children's lives. Thirdly, as a member of the local Council for Community Relations, he was committed to a philosophy of education that would steer us away from a Euro-centred approach to the curriculum towards a multi-cultural one.

Staff changes had happened naturally with his arrival. Perhaps because he found more like minds in the infant department – or maybe because he saw this as the logical starting place – this was where he decided to begin the process of change. I was to join two other teachers, Linda Cushine and Jill Wade, to form the newly created infant department of three parallel vertically grouped classes. They were family grouped so that we could forge strong relationships with families over the years as younger siblings followed on to the same teacher.

Staff meetings became a weekly feature, not just for keeping up to date with odds and ends of news, but for introducing and airing views about education in general and aspects of the curriculum in particular. As luck would have it, Reading University was running a course on new ideas which would move the stress in the teaching or reading away from a combination of flashcards and regular phonic drills towards a psycholinguistic approach of reading for meaning. As the two current infant staff were feeling disillusioned with their resources and their methods, the course seemed like the answer to a prayer. We were all very excited by what we learned, and the shared experience had the effect of making us feel like a closely knit team from the earliest days.

It cannot have been easy for established members of staff to see beliefs they felt comfortable with challenged. With hindsight this bubbly infant group, overflowing with new-found zeal, was probably overpowering in the staffroom. Possibly, a head of longer standing, with more practice in management skills, could have harnessed our energies in a more effective way. However, learning how to cope with colleagues as individuals with their own sensitivities is a very difficult task and takes time.

Another major new departure was to broaden the curriculum to include the wider world. John Shearman attacked this question on a number of different fronts. First, by looking at the books and other resources. As we bought books for our new approach to reading, we had been asked to look out for texts that reflected the multi-racial aspect of Britain. In the early seventies it was a good deal easier removing the many racist texts in use than finding suitable replacements. Later when the head moved on to writing formal job descriptions, Scale Post holders were all expected to ensure that the multi-racial dimension became an automatic consideration.

Secondly, he considered assemblies. Their format changed dramatically. They became much more vital and relevant: everyday events in the children's lives would be discussed – uncles arriving at Heathrow, new holds learned at judo, children's work shown, festivals of different religions talked about. It was no longer only the staff who could decide on the content. At the children's suggestion, there were handclapping, conker games, skipping and ball rhymes. Visitors from the immediate community and beyond came to talk to us.

Next he addressed the implications of racial diversity for the school as a whole. When a series of discussions about racial equality were organized, all staff – caretaker, cleaners, teachers, secretaries, assistants – were asked to attend, so at least everyone heard the debate, even if some were not ready to participate as yet.

Sometimes, through no careful planning on our part, cross-cultural themes would get an unexpected boost. Our peripatetic language support teacher went to India for her sister's marriage ceremony. On her return she showed us slides of the occasion and my class got carried away by it all. I have forgotten the topic I had researched for that term's work, but whatever it was it was instantly forgotten as 'our' wedding took over – in the home corner, in the dressing up corner, in art, in news time, in the library, in the children's writing. Photos and artefacts poured in from home and 'weddings' was established as the theme for the rest of the term.

When 'our' bride and groom returned to England, we invited them to visit us in school. What excitement! We made garlands, composed a musical entertainment, prepared food for a wedding feast. The children lined up to greet the couple and quite spontaneously burst into cheers and clapping as they entered. A splendid moment.

Throughout this time, the head was aiming at more open access in other directions, too. He quickly cemented a strong bond with the chairman of the governors and instigated a rota of staff to give talks to the governing body about our thinking on various aspects of the curriculum and about any innovations to the system. (This was the first of many ideas I carried forward to my next school.) For instance, Linda Cushine spoke about *Breakthrough to Literacy*,[2] Jill Wade about the library and audiovisual resources, and I talked about how an integrated day might be organized for a vertically grouped class of five to seven year olds. For how can governors be effective if they have not grasped these issues, and better still, spent time in school afterwards seeing them in action in the classroom? These sessions were quite clearly an eye opener for most governors and gave them an insight into the role of the teacher that they would otherwise have lacked. To their credit, they responded enthusiastically and there was no shortage of questions after each talk.

Opening the doors

You may think that I have taken a long time to get round to parents. Yes, I have . . . because it did! Whereas heads are absolutely crucial to any scheme that tries to involve parents, nevertheless staff are also important and, unless the head has some staff support for innovations, they will not stand much chance of success. The Infant team had certainly reached a point where we all felt secure in our relationships with one another, and where we could be totally honest in debating the educational issues. After we had thrashed out plans and policies together and got to know each other as people, then we felt ready to put into action an open door policy for parents.

Organizing social events helped us to move nearer to that goal. For instance, we hired steel bands for termly dances. At the suggestion of parents with fond memories of Caribbean carnivals, we added a street procession as an appetizer for the summer fair. (Another idea I took with me to my next school.) It was centred round a different theme each year, such as storybook characters or carnival of the animals, and all the children made costumes with the help of teachers and parents. There was a surge of community feeling as we paraded round the neighbourhood with residents smiling and waving from their doorsteps.

We wanted the old people living in the immediate vicinity of the school to feel they were a valued part of our community. After the Harvest Festival, we distributed food baskets to them, which involved children and parents making lists in advance of people who would welcome the gifts and delivering them on the day. We started a termly social evening for them, too. The PTA would escort or transport those who could not manage the walk. Food, drink and entertainment were laid on. Getting the hall ready, serving, dancing, joking, singing, clearing up afterwards was exhausting but great fun!

The Saturday 'work-in', was the first encounter with large numbers of parents coming into school. Looking back, it was probably quite a good first move. It was one step further on from the typical social event, but it was totally non-threatening, voluntary and had an obvious purpose . . . to improve the visual environment of the school. People in overalls wandered in, stayed for as long as they liked and tackled whatever jobs they felt they could handle – sandpapering, varnishing, sawing, putting up shelves. There did not seem to be a feeling that the teachers were in charge. In fact, roles were reversed as, on the whole, it was the parents who had the skills and the teachers who had to be shown what to do.

The Bullock Report added force to the argument for parental involvement and Linda Cushine was given a Scale Post with specific responsibility for liaising with parents and the community. She set up a system of home visiting, whereby every family would be visited before their child started school. In quick succession came an agreed school policy on parents in school and a series of meetings for parents of children who had just started school. The tone of these meetings left a lot to be desired as we were still labouring under the delusion that teachers, as professionals, could teach parents a thing or two about getting on with their own children!

Open evenings for parents to discuss their children's work with teachers changed in style. With shift-workers and baby-sitting problems in mind, we offered two successive evenings – one from 3.30 to 5.30 and the other from 7.30 to 9.30 – in the hope of reducing the numbers of parents who had been unable to attend in the past. We also changed to an appointment system to try to cut down the waiting time for parents. We gave a personalized appointment to every parent and it seemed to make a substantial difference.

Out of school activities increased, too, with a parent running a netball club, an older brother running a Judo club. In response to requests from parents, the head decided to keep open the playground after school for a couple of hours, as it was not safe to play in roads which were always busy with traffic. Another excellent sign that parents and teachers were working together for the good of the children was the formation of an action group from inner-town schools which led to a day conference to debate the relevant issues, and laid the foundations for the establishment of a resources centre for multi-racial education.

Who are the experts?

Although quite a few steps had been taken, parents working in the classroom were still rare. Wednesday afternoons became club time. Parents and members of the local community offered their expertise or joined classes to learn a new skill such as basket weaving, sailing, sketching. Parents offered their expertise in other ways, too. For instance, a father who ran the local Nepali restaurant showed a class round the kitchens, introducing them to all the spices and demonstrating the use of the tandoori oven.

Occasionally, special requests went out to people with specific skills such as the blind husband of one of the cleaners who came in to work on a project on the senses with the juniors. Parents helping with reading was very much by invitation only . . . but for very different reasons. Reading for meaning was new to us and, with the excess zeal of the newly converted, we wanted to ensure that everything was done just right. People who had shown an interest in our new approach to reading, people with whom we had a special rapport and whose way of engaging with children we approved of – these were the ones issued with invitations! Like many teachers experimenting in this area at that time, we failed to see the full implications of our élitist attitudes.

One anecdote I would like to share with you sums up, for me, more than any other, the importance of trust and affection between parents and teachers, and the absurdity of assuming that school can stand alone, separate from home. A five-year old arrived in my class straight from a village in Azad Kashmir, a cousin of one of our junior boys. He had been dressed in a suit and socks and shoes to which he was naturally unaccustomed. He was looked after with concern by fellow speakers of Mirpuri Panjabi in the class. Even so he was none too happy. He took off his own shoes and tried to do likewise for everyone else. By the afternoon, quiet tears of misery were running down his cheeks.

I had asked the Panjabi speakers in the class to translate everything I thought might help; I had run the gamut of smiles and gestures. There was nothing else I could think of except to clutch him to my bosom and rock him to and fro. One thoughtful child turned the pages of the book for me at story time as I whispered the story so as not to wake the now sleeping child. I was not sure what to do at home time when his cousin came to collect him. I really do not know why I did not think of carrying him home myself. Instead I sent a message home that he was fast asleep and that I did not want to wake him in case he felt frightened by his surroundings when he woke. His grandfather arrived almost immediately and carried him off home.

Next morning, the child's mother brought him into the class-room. I gestured for her to join us and she sat next to me while I took the register and talked with the class about their morning's work. It was a most unusual fifteen minutes. She started talking in her mother tongue as soon as I started talking in English and when I stopped she stopped. Her son looked delighted. The rest of the class, wide-eyed, gazed first at me and then her, their heads swivelling like centre court spectators at Wimbledon. I panicked momentarily after five minutes wondering whether it would go on like that forever. When I rose to let the children get on with their work, I beckoned to her to come and join her son and encouraged her to help him with his colours.

To my delight, she appeared next morning and the next and the next, and helped her son with sequencing bead patterns, jigsaw puzzles and Lego. She never again talked in unison with me but sat for the most part quietly by my side, launching the odd sentence here and there. Eventually she stopped coming and I assumed that she felt her son could stand on his own two feet by then. Of course, she was quite right.

This was a special, by no means isolated, incident. Parents have a unique bond with their children that no teacher, however affectionate and well-intentioned, can possibly match. In the face of such evidence, I fail to see how schools can do anything but welcome parents in.

Not only but also . . .

Anything that helps to show people in a multiplicity of roles is for the good, I feel, and that applies to teachers just as much as to parents. As I got to know the parents, I was able to switch from teacher to consumer and call on their expertise by employing them as pastry cook, builder and so on. A couple of cameos: André's beam of pride for his mum as he showed me into their kitchen where a beautifully decorated birthday cake and a tray of eclairs were waiting for me to collect for my son's birthday; Peta on the swing, playing while her father laid a new set of paving stones in our back garden.

I have always enjoyed interweaving my life at home and at school so that I am seen as a whole person – wife and mother, as well as teacher. I had been entertained in children's houses on the home visit and it seemed a natural step to invite the children to my home in return. When interesting activities cropped up at weekends, we made arrangements with parents to meet and ferry children to, say, the town bookshop for signings by children's authors. I would have been taking my own children in any case, so it was no hassle to take some extra ones.

I am quite convinced that this interest and involvement outside school time does a lot to make parents see that teachers' feelings for their children are deep and lasting. I am not suggesting that teachers have to spend every spare moment socializing with the children and their families but the occasional mixing of teachers' home and school commitments reaps benefits for all concerned.

Seeing for ourselves

Two significant events altered the quality of relationships for the better. The first was that John Shearman was awarded a travel bursary for a five-week tour of Barbados and St Vincent, the Caribbean islands where most of our West Indian families came from originally. There was much liaison with families before the visit, messages to be carried, relatives to be described, a lot of excitement about the whole project. On his return, there were slides to be shown, stories to tell, a twin school to write to and some years later a visit to Barbados from some children in the school, thanks to the financial support of local firms.

The second significant event came about because the population of the local community shifted to include many more families from the Indian subcontinent. Linda Cushine and I decided to tour India and Pakistan to find out more about these areas. Parents began to appear in school wanting to find out why we were going to their country without visiting their relatives. The whole character of the tour changed. We were seen as a physical link for the Reading families with their relatives back home. Our final itinerary was totally different from our original plan but far more meaningful for us and the families of the children we were teaching.

We spent a great deal of time sorting out dates and arrival times, talking about the people we were going to meet, looking at photo albums. The whole atmosphere altered. We felt we were real friends. The excitement was electric as children dashed into school waving letters as yet another detail was finalized. Children began teaching us Urdu words and one mother came after school to teach us some basic phrases. Monolingual children became keen to learn Urdu, too. This experience made us see more clearly the enormous educational potential of linguistic diversity in the classroom.

During the three months in the sub-continent, we learnt much about the history, the language and the culture of the people we met. It was an unforgettable experience. All too often it is assumed that emigration brings nothing but rewards. Yet one aspect in particular that struck us with force was just what people give up when they are uprooted and come to live in Britain. The loss of daily interactions within an extended family alone is an enormous price to pay. When we left Delhi, Rani, one of the children's aunts, clung to us, weeping, 'Please tell my father I miss him so much'. Images like that never fade.

Warts and all

Not everything we tried was a success. We fitted out a special parents' room and took pains to make it as attractive as possible. For a time, it was used as a meeting place, an escape from the isolation that having a young family can bring. However, a nursery unit had been built in the playground and parents seemed to think of that as a more natural meeting place, so the parents' room became redundant.

All too often in those days, schools included a passing assembly on festivals such as Eid or Diwali, or had children make an Indian dish in cookery lessons, without thinking more deeply about the implications of cultural diversity across the whole curriculum. Sometimes our desire to welcome parents into school gave rise to such criticism. When a grandmother arrived to show us how to put on a sari, there was a genuine buzz of interest from the class. On another occasion, a child brought in her mother's sari especially for me to wear at the summer fair and I accepted with pleasure. As these were not isolated incidents, it did not occur to us that they might be interpreted as tokenistic nods in the direction of multi-cultural education.

Things seemed to be going very well when one small chalk mark, a piece of racist graffiti, spotted when on playground duty, heralded a quite unexpected turn of events. The chalk was easy to wipe out but not the nasty taste it left in the mouth. A deputation of parents duly arrived at the head's office to protest their concern that blacks were being favoured at the expense of white children. Seeing this incident in its most positive light, it must have taken a lot for those parents to come forward and it did them credit that they came to school to talk the matter through instead of complaining behind our backs.

It took a lot for the head not to crumble under the disappointment but to step back and take a serious look at our policies and practices, to see where we had gone wrong for such a protest to occur and to work out how best to re-establish good relations. The Annual General Meeting (AGM) of the PTA was at hand. At that meeting the head put the case for multi-racial education with vigour, stressing that it benefits everyone, black and white alike. No one could hope to eradicate prejudices and dispel anxieties in one brief meeting, but it must be right to face up to any conflict of philosophy between home and school rather than pretend it does not exist.

Taking stock

By the end of the seventies, where were we in our thinking? There had been no lack of enthusiasm nor of a strong desire to succeed, but we lacked a well-structured plan. We were learning as we went along, in effect. The deficit model of language development still held sway. Teachers held the reins as far as the core curriculum was concerned and, for the most part, parents came into school only at the express invitation of the teachers. But, although we had not always foreseen the implications, we had not shied away from difficulties when they arose. We had realized that a genuine feeling of understanding between home and school goes a long way and that parents of all cultural and social backgrounds were eager and well-qualified to play their part. It was at this point that I moved on to Redlands.

Parents' voices

Reminiscing ten years on . . .

Opening the doors . . .

- People were inhibited in the early 1970s – you daren't just go into schools to discuss things. So when the new head came, I loved the way he and the staff made parents feel that it was their right to be there, to know about every facet of their child's education.

- It was nice not to be frightened of a headteacher. I thought John Shearman was great. He got them all in – the young and the old and they all thoroughly enjoyed it. The atmosphere got so friendly. You always felt invited and were willing to help.
- You could say what you honestly felt. Even if John thought the opposite, he would always listen to you. He never shouted you down in an authoritarian manner. We had some horrendous arguments but there was never any ill-feeling afterwards. You walked away and it was all OK and, next time you met, you were friends again.
- With the staff you could sit down in the class and ask anything about teaching and they'd lend books or take the trouble to explain.
- The friendships we built up then are still going strong even though a lot of the families have moved away. The bonds are there. Not just the parents, either. The kids still meet.
- The social aspect was great. I got to know far more people than I ever would if I'd just had to stand and wait outside the school gate.
- It was a good idea to open the playground after school, because there's nowhere round here to play. There was no bother. If you respect the kids, they respect you.

Social events . . .

- I like the old folks 'dos' the best. They did appreciate that, didn't they? They began to associate themselves with the school, then they supported the other things we did.
- I loved all the dances. They were so well attended. You could feel people were having a good time. It was good to see all the West Indian families. It's good to mix, I always think.
- Do you remember all those hours getting ready for the procession? What a lot of fun, though. Hard work for the teachers I expect. Everybody came out of doors. It was like a carnival.
- It finished up with the whole family involved. My husband on his day off – he'd have to go and borrow a lorry for the procession. My brothers would come on a visit and they'd get roped in – it was a whole family venture.

- The art classes on club day! There were about ten of us, I think. We were all hopeless, but Mrs Nicholls was lovely. We did papier mâché, pottery and drawing – nobody was brave enough to do painting. I'd always fancied myself as a bit of an artist – my son was good at art and I felt it gave us something in common when I went to art class. I liked the companionship, the friendship – not many of us worked then, so we needed that.

- When we had the parents' clubs, I did batik. My piece ended up as backing for the piano! But often we did things to sell at the bazaars. We did thousands of clay Mr Men plaques to sell once.

- John Shearman made us realize the fabric of the school was important. It hadn't been painted for a very long time. We came in and did our own thing for an hour, two hours, all day, whatever we could manage. I helped with the display boards. That day was nice and it was good to have plenty of fathers in for a change.

- I got satisfaction from 'doing my bit'. The things we did – ten mile walks in the pouring rain, forever knocking on doors and asking for things, sending begging letters to local firms. We did things for the school that we'd never have done in any other situation. There was such a feeling of involvement – parents and teachers all working together for the first time.

The wider world . . .

- I felt they went a bit over the top about religion. It was a good thing to have Ramadan and Diwali but the nativity play went, and the hymns for Harvest. I think we should have kept them so that everybody was included. I never said that to the head. I don't know why . . . I didn't think it was my place . . . but I should have done!

- Getting the book ready for the school in Barbados was great fun. The one that came back from Barbados aroused more interest in the parents though, I think. Everybody was keen to see that.

Warts and all . . .

- We tried curriculum evenings on maths, English and then the new maths. I'm sure people were really interested but then the idea of an official talk put them off. We tried to break down that barrier but didn't manage it really.
- I think we wanted the parents' room to be a drop-in centre. We tried to be there with the kettle on for people. We had a little library and you could swap paperbacks. I think we wanted to make sure that the next lot of parents would always feel welcome in the school. As parents got more involved in the school, they didn't need the room anymore.

Chapter 6

Moving on to Redlands: the PTA

It was on my return from the Indian subcontinent in 1980 that I was appointed as deputy head to Redlands School. Redlands is a tall, imposing Victorian building at the end of a cul-de-sac, buried in a maze of narrow streets with rows of terraced housing. There is a high proportion of owner occupiers. Most homes have been extended and modernized; they are well-maintained and decorated and have carefully tended small front gardens. An interesting neighbourhood. The population has changed over the years and indigenous families have been joined by families from the Caribbean and the Indian subcontinent, especially Moslems from Pakistan plus a smaller number of Hindus and Sikhs.

The school catchment area extends, on one side, to include some wider avenues with large Victorian semis and detached houses, several university halls of residence and accommodation for mature students and their families who come from abroad to take further degrees. On the other side, there are several houses converted to bed and breakfast accommodation as temporary housing for social services, and a refuge for women and children. There is thus a breadth of cultures, sub-cultures, of languages and dialects thriving in the school. Numbers on roll fluctuate from year to year but currently stand at 222, plus 40 half-time children who attend the nursery.

Like many inner-city areas, there is nowhere for children to play in the immediate vicinity of the school. Some play bat and ball games in the road and ride around on their bikes. There are two parks, but both involve a fifteen minute walk and you need to cross busy roads to reach them. If you believe that ideal conditions – a modern, purpose-built school, superbly equipped amid green pastures in a middle-class catchment area – are necessary before change can be contemplated, you will detect from this description of the school and its immediate vicinity, that Redlands does not fit that category.

Before the appointment of Michael Richards as headteacher in 1979, Redlands was typical of many primary schools of its day: an efficiently-run establishment with a body of professionals at the helm, ensuring that children had a thorough grounding, especially in the 3Rs. The emphasis was on the transmission of knowledge rather than on learning processes, with teachers as purveyors of that knowledge to children taught in streamed classes. Parents came to school only for formal open evenings to discuss their children's performance and behaviour. The outgoing head and deputy had both retired at the end of long and devoted service to the school.

Both Mike Richards and I had been at schools where parents were an important item on the agenda. We both felt that a friendly disposition and a will to forge good relationships were the most important assets for promoting change and we planned to put our accumulated experience to good use at Redlands. The new head spent some five years at the school before moving on to his next appointment. By this time, the process of change was well underway.

His successor, Mary Martyn-Johns, was appointed in 1984. She had been the teacher in charge of the Language and Intercultural Support Service (LINCS) which had worked closely with schools in the area and she was therefore well-known to the staff of Redlands and highly respected and liked by us all. She was also very much in tune with the way in which our thoughts had been developing and, because she was experienced in management skills, she has been the ideal person to take our development further.

Falling rolls in the early 1980s meant fewer staff. By 1982, only two of the original staff were still teaching in the school. Many of the present staff have been teaching at Redlands for five years, get on very well together, share the same broad views on education and debate the issues openly and honestly – thanks to the influence of those two key figures: Mike Richards and Mary Martyn-Johns.

Putting the family in the picture

As soon as Mike Richards arrived in 1979 he began to make his mark. He had a special quality, an easy-going natural manner that made it easy for him to make relationships quickly and with people of all walks of life. He had that rare ability to know how to communicate with staff, bank managers, cleaners, academics, shopkeepers, anybody and everybody. He knew how to make them feel at ease, more than at ease, in fact – valuable, liked and important. Allied to this was his own strong family feeling. Because of this, he knew, without having to make a conscious policy about it, that other parents cared deeply about all aspects of their children's lives, including their education. He felt that parents had the right to know what went on in school and to become involved in it, should they wish to be so.

As the bell rang at five to nine, he would be there without fail at the entrance, greeting children and parents. And again as the children were collected at half past three, he would be there, gradually getting to know the families better and better as the days went by, remembering the little details they told him and asking them the next day about the outcome. He did this not as part of a deliberate plan to win parents over, but simply because he enjoyed their company and was genuinely interested in them as people in their own right.

I am not suggesting that only 'special' people can forge links with parents nor, indeed, that schools have to wait for a certain sort of head before they can take action. What I am saying is that, at that moment in time at Redlands, things were made much easier for us by the head being the sort of person he was.

The close rapport between the head and the caretaker, Pete Alder, also contributed a great deal. The caretaker had lived in the neighbourhood all his life and knew the history of every family. His opinion of the new head would have spread rapidly to all who knew and admired him in the community. He encouraged parents to take jobs as cleaners and as dinner controllers when they fell vacant. He was also a key figure in the staffroom, an equal partner in the life of the school, joining in staff social events.

From listening to talking

One of the first areas of change with the arrival of the new head in 1979 was the parent-teacher association. In this respect, developments in Redlands have mirrored, by and large, the national pattern. Of the various recommendations made in the Plowden Report (1967), the one which gained ground most rapidly nationwide was the development of the parent-teacher association. It is not difficult to understand why. PTAs were concerned mainly with social activities and fund-raising events and as such they were more or less independent of the day-to-day life of the school. Their brief was definitely not to investigate central educational issues such as the school's language policy or staffing ratios. In other words, they posed no threat to teachers in their professional role.

Accounts from parents with children in the school during the seventies suggest that the PTA at Redlands, like many other schools, had been run along formal lines with the headteacher in the chair and firmly in control of the agenda. The committee members were nominated, seconded and duly elected at the AGM. Most of them came from middle-class backgrounds and nearly all of them were men. Under Mike Richards, the PTA had a new lease of life. In order to involve more people, parents were automatically eligible for the PTA committee instead of having to be elected.

Mike Richards' relaxed manner and open approach succeeded in breaking down formal barriers. The friendly atmosphere led to parents gaining a great deal in confidence. As a matter of course, before meetings closed everyone was asked in turn if there was anything further they wished to discuss, however trivial or momentous. Every contribution was seen to be valued and taken seriously.

Mike also saw PTA meetings as an ideal channel for sharing information about the school's aims, policies and resources. He had realized that keeping parents in the dark could create uncertainty, confusion or tension. Parents were far more likely to give their support if they were kept in the picture about what was going on.

He remained as president but left the chair to be occupied by an elected parent. It was a move forward, though in reality, president and chairman worked as a partnership, and I think it is doubtful whether anything would have been passed without the head's say so. Certainly when it came to spending the money earned, it was assumed that staff would make the decision and the PTA committee would hand over the cheque.

The situation has progressed even further since Mary Martyn-Johns was appointed in 1984. The composition as well as the size of the committee has changed. It is virtually 100 per cent women (men fulfilling the baby-sitting role on committee nights but lending their support for PTA events) and all sections of the catchment area are represented on it. About fifteen to twenty parents regularly attend the monthly meetings. Decisions are now based on democratic group discussions. Parents are much more likely to make suggestions, recommendations, even demands, and complaints.

For example; the first fund-raising event I was involved in was a 'Sponsor a Book' for the newly established library. The idea was readily accepted by the parents, who chose from a selection of new books ordered by the staff. A sponsored event for the infants in 1986, however, was somewhat less successful. It was a vocabulary game that involved the children in remembering as many alternative words as possible for 'said' (e.g. shouted, whispered, muttered). My phone did not stop ringing the evening the letters went out to parents. For a start, the letter had not been worded carefully enough, nor the whole event discussed sufficiently with the children. Hence they interpreted it as a sort of spelling test.

Facing up to our mismanagement was one thing, but the other point raised by concerned parents was one that neither the staff nor the PTA committee had thought of. The stated aim for the sponsorship event was to raise money to replenish our book stock. Children had somehow got hold of the idea that unless they learnt the words the new books would not be forthcoming, which put them under some strain. For some parents the very idea that children should have to perform in order to buy the very lifeblood of education was anathema. Obviously we were dismayed at having caused such a furore but very pleased that parents felt able to speak up and point out implications that we had failed to spot.

Nowadays PTA meetings devote less time to organizing events and more to educational concerns. It is not merely a case of teachers presenting information to parents or raising issues which *they* wish to be aired. At every meeting issues currently relevant to the life of the school are raised by parents and teachers alike and fully discussed – changes to the school language policy, road safety, school meals, the changing pattern of secondary education in the area, transport problems to secondary school – so that the agenda for a PTA meeting looks very much like the agenda for a governors' meeting. In fact, there is a close rapport between the two bodies and they work well together on all issues.

Although we do not always get things right the first, second, or even the third time, we have had some resounding successes. One obvious example is school meals. It was a parent who went on the school's behalf to a talk given by a dietician. She reported back the findings and set in motion the campaign to raise awareness not only among our families but also at school-meals headquarters about the importance of a healthy diet. After a lot of time and effort, this has resulted in a major transformation of the eating habits of the children, in and out of school – they are ever vigilant for suspicious E numbers on crisp packets and yoghurt cartons! It was thanks to such a vociferous campaign from the PTA and the governors that the head was able to obtain our own school kitchen on the premises, with a grandmother from the local community in charge.

Parents as purse-fillers

When I first came to Redlands, Mike Richards felt we performed something of a civic duty by removing people's rubbish for our jumble sales! He instilled in us that we must never refuse anything no matter how cumbersome, or it would reflect badly on the school's image in the community. Anyone who has collected jumble will know that it can be something of a chore if you do it on your own but, when you organize a group of parents and eager children, it is much more fun. The whole thing becomes a family affair. For although jumble sales are quite clearly fund-raising events, there is also an important social aspect to this kind of PTA activity.

The Summer Fair was rejuvenated, too, with the addition of a procession round the streets. This has developed over the years, with more and more parents being involved, coming into school as a group to work with children on costumes and decorations. Last year saw a new development, when a group of musical parents formed a band to lead the marchers. The Christmas Fair has gathered a touch of sparkle, as teachers, caretaker and children convert a store cupboard into a grotto. Two parents dress up as pantomime characters, take the money and entertain the children queueing up to see Father Christmas.

Whenever there have been worries that funds were running low, someone – usually a parent – has come up with an idea: a weekly Bingo session attended by some parents and children but also many old people in the locality; a share club; a thriving weekly second-hand clothes stall.

It was also parents' initiative that set in motion that children should make a contribution, and so the sponsored events came into being. They have followed the usual pattern – swim, walk, word search, things beginning with 's', how many things can you fit into a match box . . . and, of course, the ill-fated vocabulary game.

Again it was a parent who brought up the matter that we always raised funds for own own school and never for anything else. Ethiopia was in the news at the time, so the consensus of opinion was that we should do something as a school to help. Children and parents took on the job of raising money in many small imaginative ventures. Since that time we have kept a yearly commitment to fund-raising for an outside organization, being careful, for the sake of the hidden curriculum, to avoid choosing a third world charity every time.

Increasingly the feeling has become one of 'This is our school': so let's get our heads together and make sure it will not be short of finances when they are needed. The ambiance before, during and after an event is always hectic but cheerful. I doubt if a stranger happening upon the occasion would be able to tell who were the parents and who were the teachers from the amount or type of work they do.

Enjoying each other's company

Instead of thinking of only fund-raising events, the committee has organized evenings to enjoy being together – a display by the Milk Marketing Board, skittles at a local pub, a visit to a television

73

studio. More popular, though, were the school-based social events for the family which were introduced by Mike Richards: the Guy Fawkes Disco in the autumn and the Mad Hatter's Disco in the spring, where the main hall was used for dancing and the infant hall laid out with tables and chairs for refreshments; a barn dance in the summer and beetle drives in the winter. The latest parent initiative was a sort of old-time musical evening, very well supported by families and the local people, where parents and children performed on piano, cello, trumpet and recorder. To make sure that as many people as possible take part in organizing the events we have a standard slip that goes out to all children. The head and PTA secretary ensure that all offers to help are taken up and no one is missed out by default.

PTA events have not always been completely trouble free. For instance, we have had to weather some storms at the discos when teenage children monopolized the dance floor with their break dancing routines . . . too dangerous when sharing the limited space with three-year olds. The matter was fully debated at a PTA meeting and the decision arrived at was a democratic one. For a time, the rule stood that children must be accompanied by parents and that seemed to have solved the problem.

There has since been an interesting parents' initiative which has led to the removal of discos from the PTA social calendar for the time being. It gradually – or maybe suddenly – dawned that although families came to the disco together, they did not stay together. Parents tended to sit and chat in one area, leaving their children dancing in another, such that the teachers' role became supervisory rather than participatory.

Perhaps more importantly, though, parents realized that while the school curriculum had expanded to embrace the wider world perspective, the PTA events stemmed almost entirely from Anglo-Saxon cultural norms – Guy Fawkes disco, Valentine disco, barn dances. We had organized an international evening in the early eighties, but had given up that idea for fear of being tokenistic. Since then we had made sure that non-alcoholic drinks and Halal food were always available, plus a variety of international dishes, yet we had failed to consider the very nature of the events themselves.

However, at the start of the school year 1987–8, the AGM of the PTA had at the top of its agenda the need to counteract this pattern and to organize events that will attract all of our families. Belatedly we have realized that letters home, even in the mother tongue, are not the ideal solution for people whose culture values highly the oral tradition: direct invitations are a more effective way of letting people know what is taking place. Only by encouraging parents and teachers from all cultural backgrounds to express their views do we feel that we will find the answers.

One social activity which has worked well in attracting parents from many different backgrounds is the termly meeting where 'old' parents meet and welcome newcomers. To begin with this was simply a coffee morning. Later it shifted to the afternoon, gradually evolving into something more ambitious. Sometimes it has taken the form of a demonstration: on one occasion we had a session on tapestry given by a mother and grandmother team, and on another a knitting machine demonstration. More often, though, the meetings have centred round a cooking and eating session, to celebrate a national or regional dish.

As ever, one thing leads to another. The tradition of cookery demonstrations led one parent-cum-professional chef to organize an Easter stall to sell her homemade hot cross buns and decorated eggs. That, in turn, led to some talented seamstresses meeting one afternoon a week in the term prior to the Summer and Christmas Fairs to design and sew a wide range of items to sell at the craft stall.

In short . . .

Parents have taken an increasingly active role in the PTA at Redlands. By making meetings more informal and doing away with elections for the committee the PTA has become more attractive to a much wider range of parents. Far more women take part in the planning and they come from a wide variety of social and ethnic backgrounds. It has to be admitted that Asian parents are still under-represented but this has started to change and hopefully will continue to do so.

The greatest part of PTA time is still spent organizing activities which raise almost as much money as the school's capitation allowance. Anyone who is aware of the current trend in state education towards a two-tier system (LEA supported or LEA and parent supported), while abhorring the need for it and fighting for a

75

larger education budget from the state, can only be thankful for the contribution parents make. The difference for a small inner-town school like Redlands is staggering.

Nevertheless, as we have seen, there is more to parental involvement than purse-filling! The social aspects of PTA activities make it possible not only to forge good relations between parents and teachers but between parents themselves and with the wider community of which the school forms a part. In an atmosphere where parents and teachers can talk honestly in the confidence that people will be prepared to listen to what they have to say, the subjects of discussion are no longer limited to how the jumble will be collected, or what arrangements need to be made for the Summer Fair. Parents now expect to decide how the money they raise will be spent; staff use the meetings as a platform for disseminating information on recent ideas in education; parents feel free to express support or concern on all matters that affect the life of the school.

Parents' voices

Changes over the years . . .

- I went to Redlands as a child. I hated it. My mum and dad said the only ones that passed the 11-plus were the ones whose parents were on the parent-teacher committee. School was stiff and starchy in my day. It's much more democratic now.
- The PTA goes back a long way and a parent-teacher committee even before that. I remember we had to pay 5p a week at one time. It was always the same people involved in it. The main change came with Mike Richards in 1979. He really hit it off with the chairman of the PTA and the whole thing became a lot more open and less regimented.
- We saw Mike as an agent for change and we wanted to give him our full support. We were proud of the changes and of the new ethos of the school, the wonderful atmosphere. We were proud because the parent body as a whole contributed to that.

The committee

- I like the fact that everybody who wants is automatically a member of the PTA committee. I would never have joined if I'd had to stand for election. A lot more people are involved by doing things this way.
- The committee now, for all intents and purposes, is all female. Some people see this as a disadvantage. I disagree. The meetings are generally non-aggressive and we achieve a lot.
- We really must make sure that the PTA reflects the cultural diversity of our catchment area. We are making some progress but still have a long way to go.

The meetings . . .

- There were two things uppermost in our minds when Mike Richards arrived: fund-raising for the school and support for the head. Most ideas came from the head and the staff. The parents were responsible for one or two innovations in raising money, but the real driving force was Mike. He was the leader and we were quite happy with that.
- The PTA committee meetings have changed dramatically in content. When I first joined the committee we spent the whole time talking about fund-raising. In fact, it could take an hour to decide who would be baking the buns for different events. I found this incredibly boring and was determined to take as much as possible of that out of the meetings. Of course, a lot of time has to be given to logistics, but now we also talk to the staff about the curriculum and we have some lively interchanges.
- I think the main job is to do the fund-raising rather than discuss what goes on in school. That's important and I'm not saying that it shouldn't be discussed, but not at the PTA meetings. That should be at a different meeting because the meeting goes on so long and takes up too much time.
- When people realize what an open and friendly relationship we have with staff they immediately warm to the occasion.
- The meetings are too free and easy, maybe, and we tend to get side tracked. But having said that, I still think the PTA is run beautifully.

- I've got an evening job, so I miss a lot of meetings. I like to go whenever I can. I like to know what's going on.

Fund-raising events

- We got involved up to our necks in the library. That was the thing we were most proud of. That made more difference than anything to the life of the school. And, of course, it could be *seen* that we were achieving something. It had a snowball effect and we got a lot more parental support.
- My first reason for joining was duty. Then I found it was fun. I do sometimes get a bit niggled but I love the fairs and jumble sales. I moan a bit but I'd miss not doing it.
- Fund-raising is extremely hard work and many parents give up a lot of time and energy to do it. In an area like ours, people can often give their time more easily than their money – although at times, I wish that we could all just put in a few quid and forget the jumble sales. Having said that, of course, the jumble sales and fairs are fantastic community events. We all work hard for the money we earn but it is worth it. There is great community spirit and the co-operation of staff and parents makes the school special.
- I enjoy the jumbles. It's fascinating what people buy. Some of them come in as if it was Marks and Spencer and we were real shop assistants. It's a good laugh.
- My husband and I are game for anything so we thought we'd dress up in weird and wonderful things while they were waiting to see Father Christmas. It just took off. People look forward to it now. They start asking us what we're going to be this year. It's lovely seeing the smiles on people's faces as they walk towards you in the hall. You even get people to smile who hardly smile at all.
- I like doing the summer procession. All the people come out and they like waving and looking at us. The school's a bit out of the way, not easy to find, so it puts us on the map – they know we're still there.
- Everyone looks forward to our procession. They all come out and wave. 'Here they come again!' I expect they say. There's the head and the deputy at the front, dressed up in a sheet

or whatever. The children see them as human. It's all good fun.

Social events

- We make big efforts to have several events that are more of a social occasion than fund-raisers, though – because they are now popular family occasions – they have, in fact, started making a profit. The beetle drive has always been popular with the children and we have encouraged more adult participation by adding an indoor barn dance in autumn to the long established open air one in summer, as well as a musical evening with performances from children, staff and parents. I personally find that these social occasions are some of the most satisfying PTA events.
- We do not like our children to have so much freedom from the beginning, especially the girls. In the evenings, social events are mixed for girls and boys at the school. We would like to have some separate events sometimes for girls and boys. We worry, you see. We do not want our children to take the wrong path.
- I like getting involved on the social side. It's good to see the staff there, too. It wouldn't be the same if it was just parents and not many staff.
- My children really enjoyed the barn dance, especially dancing with their teacher. It's good for them to see their teacher at 8 o'clock at night in a different dress. It makes them more human. They see they're not just a 9 till 3.30 person.
- It's a shame we never have an adults only barn dance without any kids.
- The tea afternoons are a real help for new parents. You get to know other families and you settle into the swing of things.
- I like the idea of the tea afternoon at the beginning of term. I didn't know many people when we moved so that was very important for me. Other parents made a point of welcoming us new ones.
- I'd like to see more Asians in our tea afternoons. I still feel it's them and us.
- I like being involved with the tea afternoons. A lot of mothers

work now but I am free so it's OK for me to go in and demonstrate some cooking.
- I have had some very happy times – PTA meetings, barn dances, teas, musical extravaganzas have all been great.

Current concerns . . .

- Obviously we shouldn't have to fund-raise – educational essentials should be entirely state funded. But more and more we provide the essentials. Now, more than ever, the chief function of the PTA is fund-raising. I wish it didn't have to be this way. I'd like to provide the luxuries and embellishments but as it is we buy most of the computer equipment (when the government says it's dedicated to developing technological education). We also buy the books, for goodness sake!
- I hope that this government doesn't wreck things. I can already see the seeds of discontent creeping in. Because teachers' attention has been made to focus on how many hours they spend doing various different activities, there's a very strong temptation for them to think twice about attending 'non-educational' events like jumble sales which they have automatically supported in the past. These divide and rule tactics could easily destroy what we've created.
- I would hope for political change so that we could build on our relations with the school and not have to spend all our time raising funds to pay for what we consider to be important.
- Sometimes I wonder. There's an awful lot of talk, but what actually gets done? Take that crossing for the children – we've been on about that for years.
- I think the dinners are good now. We are satisfied. My son has fish and vegetables and dessert. We know it's alright for us. We know you use Halal food.
- For the last year, I have been writing letters and making phone calls about getting a decent bus service for kids from our area travelling to secondary school. I got precisely nowhere. Now that the PTA has taken it on as an issue, we've arranged a public meeting, written to councillors, raised a petition and lobbied a council meeting. Finally it looks as if we are making some real progress.

Children's voices

Fairs . . .

- For the Summer Fair I was Cinderella in the parade with a hat like a king wears, only taller, and I think I had a wand. It was good because I had a choc ice and a lolly after. And people took photos of us.
- I like my mum doing the face painting because sometimes she lets me have a free go. It washes off, you know. You only have to put soap on.
- The summer fairs are definitely very good compared with the other schools I know. It changed completely when they moved to having it outside. It was like a party atmosphere then.
- My brother doesn't want to go in the parade sometimes. I loved it – I had lipstick on my face all round. My mum got time off work to come.
- The wet sponge throwing was my favourite. It gave you a wonderful sense of doing something you shouldn't – especially when it was a teacher! Soaking my dad a good few times wasn't bad either!
- My mum played the drum and my dad played the violin in the procession. I'm learning the recorder in school and then I can play, too.
- My mum's got an important job to do at the discos – she serves drinks and things. I like the flashing lights.
- Well, I think I like the discos best because they're nice and lively . . . and the Christmas Fair because there's loads and loads of things to do.
- We used to wait to see Father Christmas. My little brother got a toy car and my sister got a little doll and I got a ball. And I bought some earrings and five cakes.
- At the Fair, my mum worked on the tombola stall. She was selling the tickets. We tried to win something but we didn't.
- My mum made some snowmen's heads for the ends of pencils and some pirates for the Summer Fair, and some matchboxes with felt on to keep your treasure in.

Jumble sales . . .

- When we got home from the jumble sale we had two big black bags full of stuff.
- I like the jumble sales because you can buy lots of books and toys.
- I had £5 to spend once. Not 5p. £5!
- I like the jumble sale best because there are so many things that you've never seen before . . . like china things. I collect china things.

Winning prizes . . .

- My favourite was when I went to the beetle drive. I won a box of chocolates. It had purple and gold wrapping.
- My mum used to do the Bingo teas and I used to go then. You could win money and a raffle. I won a bag of apples once. We only go at special times now, like Christmas.

Chapter 7

Opening the doors

The crucial recommendation of the Plowden Report was that schools needed to make themselves more accessible to parents. Only when barriers between teachers and parents had been overcome would it be possible to achieve better educational results for all children. One way of breaking down barriers was through the work of parent-teacher associations. The Plowden Report (1967) suggested other ways, too, including meetings for new parents, meetings to discuss children's progress and home visits.

In the years following Plowden, the emphasis changed considerably as the various parent groups made it clear that good channels of communications were essential. The 1980 and 1986 Education Acts – partly in response to parental pressure and partly, no doubt, for the government's own political ends – have put the notion of accountability firmly on the agenda. The governing body has to report to the parent body on developments in the previous twelve months; all LEAs are also required to give parents information on schools and all schools prepare booklets giving details about organization, curriculum, school rules and policies.

In spite of the recommendations of the Plowden Report (1967) and the plethora of reports that followed in its wake, despite the legal backing of the recent Education Acts, communication between school and home varies considerably from one school to another. Legislation can only take us so far. Goodwill on the part of parents and teachers alike is needed in large doses to enable a smooth and useful relationship to develop.

Of course, many schools throughout the country – and Redlands is one of them – have been working towards open access and good communication with parents for many years quite independently of any legislation.) When the new head, Mike Richards, arrived at Redlands in 1979, his experience in his previous schools had made him feel that, as a professionally trained body, the staff had a duty to explain to parents what we were aiming for in educational terms. To do so, we obviously had to get parents into school. The question was how to set about it. It never occurred to us that parents might be ready to rush in, if only teachers would open the portals! Our intention was to start small and hope to expand gradually.

First impressions

We knew that to make parents feel welcome in the school we had to make ourselves accessible. As I have said, the new head had made it his policy to stand at the school entrance every morning and again at home time. We hoped we had made it clear that parents were allowed inside the school and that the most comfortable place to wait for children, certainly in cold or wet weather, was inside not outside the building. We had to make sure that 'inside the building' was a pleasant place to be.

The outside appearance of the school has not altered greatly since 1980, yet there are significant changes if you let the eye linger. A nursery unit, which opened in 1982, took over some of the lower school area inside, plus a third of the already cramped playground. The crumbling outside lavatories were pulled down to create more space. Two small flowerbeds were planted there and some bench seating installed. Trees were planted with tiny surrounding flower beds enclosed by wooden benches where children could sit and chat, away from the inevitable ball games and skipping. In summer parents find them a convenient place to gather.

There is no unsightly graffiti. I feel we owe this to the attitude and hard work of the caretaker, Pete Alder, who takes enormous pride in the school. He makes sure that the outside walls of the school are as immaculate as the ones inside and that the alleyway by the side of the school is swept free of every sort of litter each morning before the children start arriving.

The resurfaced tarmac has been livened up with coloured markings for hopscotch and the like. But the highlight is without doubt the two murals that the children painted with the help of students from the Department of Fine Art at the university and from the College of Higher Education. One is a railway station and the other 'The Elements'. It is interesting to note how these features have transformed life at playtime. Activities centre round a train journey, hot air balloon rides and magic carpet journeys to all points of the globe.

Welcome notices in several languages lead you into the school itself. A glass-cased notice board for parents originally put up for PTA announcements now has notices about the community bingo sessions, the share club and all manner of advertisements from families which result in a thriving second-hand trade. There is so much material that a second larger board has been added for parents just inside the entrance.

Once inside the school the changes are more obvious. There was no central library in 1980. Mike Richards and Pete Alder created one, ready for me on my arrival to fill with stock. They knocked out cupboards, fitted new lighting, painted the walls, ordered shelves, chairs and tables and laid carpets.

It was a boon that both head and caretaker were such keen do-it-yourself enthusiasts. Anything we wanted, they would immediately set to and provide. Large display boards sprang up in the entrance hall, on landings, in the upper and lower halls, in classrooms. As capitation allowed, new furniture was brought for each junior classroom in turn. Carpets were laid to provide every room with a book corner and a comfortable place for discussion.

Of course, we slipped up on occasion. We equipped one room as a language room for the sole use of the language support teacher as we felt it important to give it the same status as any other classroom. As thinking changed, language support work was carried out in mainstream classrooms and not in withdrawal groups, so the language room became an anachronism and reverted to being an ordinary classroom.

The small downstairs medical room was converted into an office for the secretary. This left the upstairs office for the head. He immediately refurbished it with a thick pile carpet, easy chairs and a coffee table. My first reaction was of utter amazement. Where were his priorities? The number of things we needed for the children still! How could he be spending money on his room?

I got the answer. He reminded me of the importance of first impressions and visual impact. Did it not make sense to try and improve the quality of the environment in order to encourage people to spend time in it? How much easier it would be for parents to talk to the head without vying with the noise of a typewriter or telephone conversations. How much more likely parents were to be frank without a third person in the room overhearing everything. How much more relaxed the atmosphere would be if the room looked more like somebody's sitting room instead of a head's office. Of course, he was absolutely right.

On show

We felt people were more likely to make the effort to come into school if their own child was taking part in a specific event. So class assemblies seemed as good a place to start as any. On a rota basis staff chose when they wanted their class to lead the proceedings. Invitations went out to the parents of children in the class concerned. Today the formula is less rigid and seems to work well. Whenever classes feel they have something of interest to offer to the school, they present it in an assembly and make their own decision as to whether or not to invite parents.

The Harvest assembly attracted parents, too. There had been a tradition of inviting a speaker to this festival, usually the local vicar. We decided to broaden our outlook and ask the head of the Language Support Service who had recently returned from living in the Far East to talk to us about harvesting in Hong Kong and China. (Little did we know then that she would one day be the head of Redlands!) Thus, in a small way, parents were passively witnessing curriculum change as it happened. Gradually, of course, active parental involvement increased, as we expanded the festival so that each class was responsible for making dishes from all points of the compass. One Asian mother told us in Urdu how to prepare a vegetable curry, for instance, and parents began to stay on after the assembly to help the caretaker and general assistant to pack up the parcels for elderly people in the neighbourhood and to take them out to the houses with the help of the children.

Coming at a time when everyone is full of 'goodwill towards men', the Christmas play is a big attraction. But for whom? Not for our Jehovah's Witness families. Not for our Moslem, Hindu or Sikh families. Not that is, if it is always a play to celebrate the birth of Jesus. So the performance was handed over to the music specialist. She involved the choir, recorder groups, and music club members in a musical play, more in line with the pantomimes performed at this time of year. That raised another concern: would Christian families feel ignored or undervalued? Alternatively, this course of action could have been misinterpreted as setting Christianity on a pedestal, the accepted norm that need not even be discussed as opposed to Islam, Hinduism, Buddhism or Judaism which could then be seen as mere exotica.

The solution, for once, seemed quite straightforward. Today, we hold the musical event in the second to last week of term and devote the last assembly to the Christmas story. During the last week of term infants and juniors hold carol-singing concerts for interested parents and friends. Their character has altered as time has gone by to include songs from the Caribbean, Mexico, France and Germany all sung in the original language and accompanied by the children on musical instruments. Thus, although a single faith festival, we make it a multi-lingual one.

Parents' evenings

Another development in the eighties was to introduce the two consecutive Parents' Evenings with an appointment system, exactly as at my last school. Parents had previously been queueing up by signing their names on the blackboards as they arrived, and darting from room to room if they had more than one child at the school. Now the whole staff liaise on appointment times so as to prevent parents having time-wasting gaps. There are, admittedly, hiccups. Some of us get carried away and sometimes overrun but, by and large, the system works well.

Letters inviting parents to make an appointment are sent out in mother tongue as well as English and an interpreter attends the meetings. We arrange to see parents who are unable to keep appointments at a time that is convenient for them. These instances are now a minute proportion, say two out of thirty-four children, so it is not a mammoth chore.

We have an open-door arrangement on parents' evenings. Some parents will be reading through their children's work, some will be wandering round reading displays, while the teacher talks to parents in turn. I used to worry about the lack of privacy inhibiting some parents. It does not seem to be an issue any longer although, of course, if any parents requested a confidential meeting, it would be arranged. As infant teachers have daily contact with most families, we would see them immediately if we were concerned about anything. Because of daily classroom access, parents know each other well and they are unlikely to overhear anything at parents' evenings that they did not know already. We look on these evenings now as a chance for contact with working fathers and mothers as they are the ones we do not see everyday for anything more than a hurried greeting.

The usual pattern for those evenings was for one set to take place early in the autumn term and the other towards the end of the summer term. The rationale was that the autumn ones gave teachers a chance to find out as much as possible about the children who would be in their care for the year ahead. The summer set provided a convenient moment to sum up on the year just ending. In the parents' eyes one evening was too early and the other too late to be really useful. We have tried various combinations in an effort to satisfy both parents and teachers, and this year the plan is to have meetings each term.

Seen and heard

We began to mix business with pleasure at the AGM of the PTA. The first year we introduced the new library to the parents and talked about our approach to the teaching of reading, before making way for refreshments. The next year it was the turn of the maths advisor to talk about new ideas in the teaching of maths. There was time for questions but, by and large, the parents' role was to listen and learn.

How different a picture you would get from the four curriculum evenings (on school organization, language, maths and topic work) five years later when Mary Martyn-John's influence began to be felt. There were no longer rows of chairs facing a platform in the hall but a circle of chairs in different classrooms each week and all members of staff involved in talking about some aspect of the curriculum each evening. The teachers put forward their beliefs about education and showed how we implemented them in the classroom, but this was not a one-way communication. The parents had 'hands-on' experience of different areas of the curriculum. There was constant stopping and starting and inter-ruptions for questions and airing alternative views and I feel it was the beginning of a debate, a genuine dialogue with parents about education.

Real worries were voiced by parents at the maths meeting. It did not come as a complete surprise. Although a new set of published materials had been introduced in 1981, the policy docu-ment had still to be finalized. We were aware of our shortcomings in this area and felt it was important not to fob the parents off with smiles and false promises. We agreed to make Maths the priority for the next term's in-service work and to enlist the help of the LEA's maths support team. They tailored a course especially for us, then one of the team worked a day a week alongside our staff in the classroom, helping us by example of good practice.

The last of the four meetings was on topic work and after an initial explanation of how we had set up the topic for the current term, we set about deciding on a theme for the following term, parents and staff together. It was just like a bigger version of a staff meeting. Once the theme had been decided, we brainstormed together. I acted as scribe as people shouted out ideas. I found this experience exciting and I believe the parents did, too. It was quite a step forward from being a mere consumer to having had a hand planning the term's work.

New parents

Since 1982, letters have gone out to all parents of children on the waiting list in the term before they are due to start school, asking them to come to meet the class teacher after school over a cup of tea. By then the decision has been made as to which one of the three classes each child will go into. We feel family connections are important and, wherever possible, children are placed with the person who has taught their older siblings. For placing first-born children we take into account the balance in the classes on gender and culture but we also bear in mind the temperament of the child and the teacher. Parents now have a say, too, and they can discuss the placement beforehand with the head and the infant staff.

Nursery staff, infant staff and the head are all at the New

Parents' Meeting and the parents come with or without their offspring, depending on their choice. We used to ask another teacher to run a crèche in an adjacent classroom but now feel that it is not necessary, as children play happily in the sand or on the carpet. The head explains the basic factual things about the school, such as times, PE kit, and dinner routines. She distributes the school brochure and the two school policies on sexism and racism. Other policies are at hand if required.

Between us, the infant staff run through how we approach reading and writing. We demonstrate the use of *Breakthrough to Literacy*[1] materials. We look through the boxes of books so that parents get to know our stock. We demonstrate how we teach handwriting and the alphabet, how to use the library and so on. We stress the importance of reading stories to children and of learning rhymes and songs. We also run through spatial relationships, concepts of size, length, weight, texture – all the things that parents expose children to every day on their walks, when they go shopping and when they are cooking. So on through the curriculum . . . maths, art, music, cookery, science, sewing, drama, PE, how the integrated day works and the importance of play. The emphasis has shifted considerably these days. We no longer lecture parents. It is more a question of reassuring, of reinforcing beliefs and reminding parents how crucial their role in education is. We point out that we have an open classroom policy for the start and end of the school day when we hope parents will come and look at children's work.

We do realize that it may have been difficult for some parents to make it to the meeting in the first place and not just because of family constraints. Some may have come but dreaded it. Some may have come because authority called. Some may have come anxiously wondering whether they had enough English to understand the proceedings. Some may have been horrified not to find rows of desks facing the front. There is obviously a great deal of information to assimilate in one meeting and there may well be a case for organizing things differently, but parents have certainly made it clear that they are eager to find out as much as possible.

After that New Parents' Meeting, as we call it, children spend one morning a week in their prospective classrooms for the rest of the term, prior to their starting school full-time. When parents come to fetch their children at the end of the morning they look at everything their child has done, have a quick word with the teacher and hopefully establish the pattern of always coming into the classroom and taking an interest in what their child has been doing in school.

Home visits

At each new parents' meeting we arrange a home visit with the families. We usually fit it in towards the end of the holiday so we will be fresh in the children's minds when they start school. We stagger the new intake over the first few days of term so teachers can devote more time to each individual. When I first mention the home visits to people outside the school, they often think that parents might object and see it as a way of spying on them, their home, their provision for their children and so on. Nothing could be further from the truth. The idea was to meet parents on their home ground, somewhere where they felt completely at ease and where we hoped to be accepted as persons in our own right, not just as teachers. It is the family we are interested in not the choice of curtain material and we hope it has always been understood by parents as just that.

In the early days, the LEA forms for entry to school came in handy for breaking the ice but are no longer needed for that purpose. We also have our own more detailed family record form these days, giving details of the cultural and linguistic background of everyone in the family. This helps us know who to turn to for practical assistance and advice which will ensure that cross-cultural themes are included in a positive way in the curriculum. The services of an interpreter are also available for these visits should they be needed.

Strengthening the bonds

In the early eighties, a major contribution towards forging home and school links came from Rose Larter, the teacher from the Teaching and Support Services (TASS) who worked part-time at Redlands for two mornings a week, helping children whose progress with reading had stalled. She saw any child that the head and the teachers were worried about. After a counselling session to see how the child felt, a Neale Analysis Test was given in groups. Children came to her sessions in small groups and read books together and talked informally. The accent was on reading for pleasure and the right level of book was carefully chosen so that children did not face failure. By building firm bonds, a child's confidence was increased.

Termly meetings with the head, Rose, class teacher and language co-ordinator took place to discuss strategies for the future. Parents were not automatically informed when their child joined this group until one parent took us to task about this. Now it is standard practice for the head to discuss the arrangement with parents before the child joins the group.

For parents' evenings, Rose sent out a personal letter to all parents of children in her groups. She then arranged to visit the homes of those parents who were unable to attend. She was always warmly welcomed and realized that for parents who were still at a stage when they found it difficult to go to the school for meetings, this was a happier alternative.

Another strategy of hers was to send home a notebook with each child, a message book really, to get a dialogue going with parents on a regular basis. It was not for a commentary on how the child had coped with the reading, but more for personal comments, e.g. 'I like your daughter's new hair style – looks marvellous'. Parents would often respond with their worries, in which case she would arrange a home visit and would visit regularly if she felt support was needed. She is a trained counsellor and was well aware of the importance of counselling for reading progress. Once these links were established the message books died a natural death. If any of her group moved to another area of the town and had to move schools, she made a point of visiting the head of the new school and the prospective class teacher and of visiting the family in their new home as a farewell gesture. All her parents come to see her on parents' evenings these days and with two evenings available for her small groups she can devote more time to each family than a class teacher could.

Two-way traffic

Contacts keep snowballing. Grown up children of staff have become baby-sitters for parents. One mother who has recently gone into business as a decorator has been inundated with offers of work from both parents and teachers. Another parent has come to the rescue with a sewing machine to kit me out for my holidays, and ended up teaching me how to use the machine myself. The evening before Mary Martyn-Johns and I left for a teachers' tour of Israel, a knock on the door announced the arrival of a parent bearing ear plugs because she had heard Jerusalem was noisy at night. Two parents have just started to retrain as primary school teachers. After several years using them as sounding boards for our ideas, it will be a welcome reversal to find them talking to us about their plans for the classroom.

Lending an ear

So what have we actually achieved to date? There can be no doubt as to parents' interest in, or commitment to, their children's schooling. We have learnt never to underestimate them. We started off wanting to let parents know what we were aiming at, we wanted their blessing and we were aware of the value of home and school working together, pulling in the same direction. If we are honest, we expected to influence the home to go our way. Gradually, though, we have learned that parents should be listened to, rather than talked at. If you proceed without consulting parents, you risk causing misunderstanding and confusion. If you capitalize on their interest and involve them in developments, they are enormously supportive.

Parents' voices

On feeling welcome . . .

- I went to Redlands as a child and I've had experience of five different headteachers – two when I was in school and three in the time my children have been there. Things are very different now. School used to be a closed book for parents. The kids went in, you saw them through the gate and that was it. You had no idea what was going on inside. The only reason you used to go inside the school was when you had something to complain about. You always had a good hearing and the problem was dealt with, but you would never think of going inside if it wasn't to sort something out.

- Going to school is traumatic for the parents as well as the children and if everyone is made welcome within the school this period is made easier and calmer for the whole family.
- One of the things I really appreciate is how the head is always standing there at the door as you bring the children there. She's interested in you as a person and you feel you can tell her what's going on. Sometimes when I go in feeling really down, a friendly pat or hug can make all the difference. And that friendly feeling doesn't stop with the head.
- I must admit as soon as I walked into this school, I felt involved. I've never felt like a stranger or scared – it's home from home.
- What a good thing to get to know the teacher. This makes parents very happy.
- We very much appreciate the access we have to the teachers and classrooms. I feel communications are much better than they are at many other schools. I feel welcome, as do my daughters.
- I think it's a very friendly place. Everyone is always smiling and helpful, even the headteacher. She always listens seriously to my questions and tells me the answer.
- In my children's last school, you weren't allowed past the front door and you only saw the classroom on parents' evening. Having looked after a child for five years, it's appalling to have to completely hand over their care to someone else.
- Effective parent-school relationships have to be based on mutual trust and friendship. Parents need to feel welcome in the school at all times, not simply there to deliver or collect children.
- I liked school when I was a kid but I think I enjoy it more now I'm grown up.

Assemblies . . .

- Assemblies are smashing. It gives the children confidence. I wish we'd had to do it when I was at school – I might be more confident now! It makes them more outgoing. It's good to see other class assemblies, too – I think they learn a lot from that. My son remembers it all in his head and he pours it all out for us at home.

Introduction to the school . . .

- When we came to register, the class teacher met us in the office. I knew that this was the school for us when one of the children ran in and hugged and kissed her.
- Going to the school for the first time to register my son a year or so before he was five, I thought it would be a matter of just giving name and address. In fact I ended up having an hour's chat with Mike Richards on primary school education, Redlands' neighbourhood, etc. I was struck by the fact that he knew each child and that children came up and gave him 'news' as we went around the school. I was shown the 'help-yourself' library area and told that the object was to get every child with a book in its hand as a natural event.
- I didn't bother going to the New Parents' Meeting for my second child. But for the first one – it was really good, really useful. They taught us all the new ways of doing things. It all fits into place when you get involved in the classroom afterwards.
- I remember my son's teacher greeting me in the hall with words of 'Have you seen the fantastic work Alan's done this week?' The temptation to collect your offspring and disappear was not allowed! Parental interest was fostered right from the start on a positive note. Parents shouldn't only meet teachers when there are problems. They should enjoy the good together as well as trying to tackle the problems together.

Parents' evenings

- I've no complaints. They're all so helpful, so accommodating. In the papers they're always moaning about teachers. But take parents' evenings. They're here till 8 or 9 o'clock at night. I'm sure they'd rather be with their families, wouldn't they? But there they are talking to you. I do appreciate that.

- Sometimes I worry in case I'm not getting an honest answer about my child's progress.
- I want to make sure my son's getting a fair deal, whether he's clever or not. I think they're very useful. It wouldn't be a bad idea to have a written termly report as well. It wouldn't have to say that the child came twentieth out of thirty-two like they did in our day, but they could give a clear idea of how they are getting on in different subjects.
- I want to hear true things, not just 'He's alright'. I want to see that the teacher is fair to all children. Back home everybody studies well. The teachers are very strict and there is no answering back. It is important to get a good job. I want to feel that this happens here.
- They're always very pleasant events, though I sometimes think that for parents like myself who spend a good deal of time in school, they are not altogether necessary. I see my son's work very often and I have the chance to talk to his teacher as and when the need arises.

Information on the curriculum

- Schools today are so different from when most parents went to school. It is important to educate the parents into the teaching methods of today. If the parents understand how the school works, then reading and learning at home become easier for the child. The best way for the parents to learn is to come into the school and see for themselves.
- May I suggest we have more regular information evenings – on language, maths, general policy. I personally would appreciate a talk on the forward trends in the teaching of reading.
- Now we hear sex education will come. We don't like the idea of this in school, especially not as young as the juniors and especially not girls. We don't know till we marry in Pakistan. A film for parents to see first and decide? No, I could not watch such a film. I would feel shame.

Writing home . . .

- I was really taken with the friendly way the letters were written. There is never a feeling of 'you' and 'us', but rather it's 'we're all in this together', whether it's declaring warfare on nits or talking about solutions to staffing problems. I didn't realize just how important this was until we started receiving letters from my son's secondary school. They are full of 'We expect' and 'You must' and it feels very much as if you're being handed down the Ten Commandments on Mount Sinai. My reaction to this kind of letter is to switch off completely.

- You write everything down in your culture. If you want parents to know something – a meeting, a trip, cooking money – you do everything with notes home with the kids. Well, we look at the letters and we mutter, but really we don't take much notice. You see, we do it the verbal way. We tell people. Just say to them what you want and it will be done. Don't take my word for it. Give it a try. You'll find people will do things straightaway then.

Home visits

- The first time I probably thought they were poking their nose in. But, you see, I think they should. They've got to get an idea of the home environment – are the kids fed and cared for? They've got to watch for battering. These things are important. It's more than being a teacher these days – they're like social workers as well.

- They come to ask you certain questions about your child. They look at your home and how your child is at home. This has a lot to do with children's progress when they get to school – it's not an invasion of privacy. The nursery place for my daughter came up suddenly, and the teacher called to let me know. I wasn't expecting her. Fortunately the place was tidy, but I can honestly say I wouldn't have minded anyway.

- The first time I had a home visit it was a new nursery teacher and I think it must have been more difficult for her than it was for me. The fact that she came with the deputy head helped a lot. She got very excited about crawling through

my son's play tunnel with him and this had the effect of
breaking the ice! The advantage of the home visit is that
you're seeing teachers on your own territory. It helps them
see you as a whole person rather than simply as a parent.

On resolving conflict . . .
- We discovered by chance that our son was two years behind
  in his maths and we were furious. I went to the head barely
  suppressing clouds of smoke and explained what the problem
  was. I expected her to be very defensive and to attempt to
  put the blame on the child rather than the school. To my
  surprise, she really took on board what I was saying. What
  is more, she took action to put things right: she put a
  monitoring scheme for progress in maths into action
  immediately; she made contact with the maths adviser and
  made maths the in-service theme for the term. I respond
  more warmly to this kind of response than to being fobbed
  off with excuses.
- I feel I can say what I think without sounding as if I am
  complaining all the time.
- They'll always give you a fair hearing even if they don't agree
  with you.
- If I have a problem I know I can go and talk to the head
  about it. I'll say 'My son's having difficulty with . . .'
  whatever, and we'll sit down and sort it out. In their last
  school, you would only go in if it was a major issue and
  you'd have to really psyche yourself up to go in. Here I feel
  we're working together for the child.
- I am aware that a school opens itself to criticism when it opens
  the doors to parents. I think this is very brave!

On belonging to a multi-ethnic community . . .

- I remember that there was no pussy-footing around the fact
  of Redlands having a high number of children of Asian
  parents and a similar number of children from many other
  countries on a temporary basis. Both were represented as a
  strength. In a firm but pleasant way I think the head was
  saying to me, as to all new parents, 'The school is multi-

racial, multi-cultural, multi-language and if your child comes here it is assumed that you accept these dimensions as valuable'.

- The one thing I really like as a West Indian parent is the way that no child is allowed to make a racist remark. The staff just won't stand for it.
- I was very impressed when I was helping in my son's class. They were sitting on the carpet having a serious group discussion about racism and sexism. Not only did they have all the basic concepts but they had the vocabulary to go with them.
- I wish I knew more Asian parents. At times, I think it's still like two separate worlds and that's sad.
- It's very important for me that my children go to a school where other languages and cultures are valued and respected. I feel they are very fortunate to be able to grow up understanding the fact that we're all different is something interesting, something to be proud of and not something to fear or sweep under the carpet. Just as important, they're aware that we have much more in common with each other than things which make us different.
- I want to stress this . . . we parents see the ethnic mix in the school as a definite advantage. We like all the cultures to interact and support each other. It must benefit the children.

Children's voices

On home visits . . .

- My teacher came to tea so when it was the first day of school I just rushed into the class.
- It's nice when you come to tea at our house. I showed you our new baby. She's big now. She can crawl.

On parents' evenings . . .

- My dad plays jokes on me when he goes to parents' evenings. He says he doesn't like my work, but he does really!
- It's good for the children in one kind of way. The parents

look at your work and they think you need more or less of
something and then they can help you do it. My spelling
wasn't very good and my mother could help me by doing
more reading with me.

On assemblies . . .

- We're having our assembly soon and I'm going to hold
  something up and do a bit. My mum's coming to see it all.
- I like it when parents come to assemblies. It's nice for parents
  to see their children doing things.
- It's good when parents come to assemblies. The school always
  wants photos of things to make into books and parents take
  thousands of photos.

On belonging to a multi-ethnic community . . .

- We've got a new boy in our class. He's from America. People
  come from everywhere in our school.
- My dad's finished his work at the university but we don't
  know when we're going back to Iraq, so he might come in
  and teach us some Arabic. I can write the numbers in Arabic
  from 1 to 100. It's very hard to write it. I don't know how
  to spell much yet.
- I don't think many different nationalities go to Japanese
  schools but here there are people from lots of countries. It
  doesn't matter if you don't understand.
- My daddy tells us stories at night about how he used to go to
  school. And he tells us long stories, if we're early, about
  Ravana and the fireworks and about Rama and being away
  from the Kingdom for fourteen years.
- I like it when new people come and tell me different words
  in their language.
- Our new girl is good at making things with paper and she
  does lovely drawings. She brought two balloons made out of
  paper and you could blow them up.
- I like learning Urdu in school. It's good, especially the writing.

Chapter 8

Parent governors

Parent governors are a relatively new development. Until recent years, only a small number of governing bodies made provision for a parent representative. However, with the coming of the 1980 Education Act the election of a parent to the governing body became a statutory requirement. The 1986 Education Act further strengthened the parents' position, greatly increasing the number of parent governors.

I suppose in a new and developing area, teething problems of one sort or another are inevitable. I recently spoke to a woman who had served as a parent governor in the seventies and she brought home to me very forcibly how daunting a task it must have been in those days for a lone parent governor on a governing body. 'I'm an ordinary person, a mum,' she said. 'I can tell you in a word what I felt. Fright! I knew nothing about parent governors – going through the chair and all that highfalutin' language. And the handbook . . . well, apart from the "ands" and "thes", I didn't understand a word. For two years it was totally above my head – I didn't join in at all. I was so confused with all that special wording and formal attitude. I felt I was there to make the numbers up, but I had no real power. Your voice didn't count in a crunch.'

Press reports suggest that the problems of being a parent governor have not been removed by recent legislation. There has been a great deal of discussion, for instance, about the amount of support which schools can reasonably be expected to give both candidates and elected representatives to enable them to carry out their roles efficiently; and about the importance of training if parent governors are to function as equal partners on governing bodies.

I can't speak for schools in general, but in Redlands in the early eighties there was plainly confusion about what was expected of parent governors and about the kinds of issues it would be appropriate to raise. Parent governor did not seem to be the most popular of jobs and there was no rush of volunteers to stand for election when a place fell vacant. As parents have become more involved in the life of the school, though, this state of affairs has improved considerably.

Over the years parent governors have come from all walks of life and have represented a cross-section of the school community in social if not in racial terms. The two present parent governors are both women. They have a strong voice on the PTA and are very well known to parents. Both are educated, articulate and well-versed in the ways of committees. Though both are members of different political parties, neither pursues a party line and they are seen to have the interests of the whole community at heart.

Both work at home, so are free to meet outside school and enjoy daily contact with other parents. This obviously helps in the dissemination of information. Notices are posted in good time before each meeting and a full report posted afterwards. The head has always been prepared to arrange for letters to be typed, translated, duplicated and distributed on behalf of parent governors whenever asked, which is not the case in many schools. However, most information flows by word of mouth and is dealt with as it arises, rather than being saved up for the formal meeting time.

Finding their feet

Once you become a governor information automatically comes your way from the LEA. Articles of Government and Instruments of Government are both worded in rather archaic legal language that makes for dry reading for all governors, parents, teachers and political appointees alike. To fall in line with the 1980 and 1986 Education Acts, the LEA now supplies a much more attractive booklet, 'A Handbook for Governors', with photos, a clear layout and a question and answer format, phrased in more accessible language. There is also a termly broadsheet which carries a brief résumé of current educational issues in the country, draws attention to events and courses for governors in the area and has a letters section where parent governors feature prominently. The tone is friendly and conversational.

Even so, most governors would welcome something more by way of initiation. There are courses for governors on offer from time to time, but not nearly enough and not catering for all needs and pockets. They take various forms. Sometimes they are informal workshops at teachers' centres, sometimes a series of meetings put on by the Workers' Educational Association. The Open University has also run some courses on the subject, ideal for those who find it difficult to leave the house because of family commitments. The National Association for Primary Education ran a course in the county not long ago. It consisted of a series of six weekly meetings in the evening, which posed problems for many people in terms of timing, cost (there was a fee) and transport. One good sign, however, was that they offered it to 'experienced, new and *potential* governors'.

Extending the boundaries

In the early 1980s, the parent governors saw themselves as representing the PTA committee and reported to the governing body solely on PTA functions and fund-raising events which was, of course, in line with earlier thinking on parents' place in education. In summer 1984 came the first mention in a parent governors' report of anything other than PTA concerns. It was to support a request for more dinner-time supervision in the playground. Since then they have broached many topics such as the poor standard of school meals (resulting eventually in our getting an on-site kitchen), the shortage of Educational Psychologists in the county, transport to secondary school and support for the teachers' action. At the same time as their confidence increased, so did their participation in debates at the meetings.

As LEAs and schools have become more accountable to society, so parent governors have been privy to more important discussions taking place at governors' meetings, for instance, on funding, resources, cuts, staffing, new LEA policies about corporal punishment, Section 11 funding, anti-racist education, 'special needs', and provision for secondary education in the county. In no way are parent governors marginalized. As Redlands introduced the tradition of having members of staff talk about curricular matters at governors' meetings, so parents became versed in all areas of the curriculum and are now included in all aspects of decision-making. At my interview for the deputy headship both parent governors were present. One of them was also part of a trio of governors involved in the long listing of candidates for the head-ship in 1984 and sat on the interview panel.

In an effort to increase governors' knowledge and involvement in the school, Mike Richards introduced a half-hour meeting with tea and biscuits for staff and governors before the formal meeting began. This lightened the atmosphere considerably for all concerned. Teachers and governors would wander off to browse round the classrooms and look at displays and other work. The formality of going through the chair at a meeting of this kind seems something of an anachronism. Usually a more free-discussion style is adopted, though the chair can call us to order if necessary.

The new order

According to reports in the press, the rush of special parents' meetings in July to comply with the 1986 Education Act resulted in very poor attendances for schools up and down the country – primary and secondary alike. This was not our fate at Redlands. The library was packed out and we had to hunt for more chairs to seat the audience. Almost every teacher was there, part-time and temporary as well as full-time and permanent. Ten out of twelve governors were present. To be quorate we needed 50 parents and 63 attended the meeting, representing a good cross-section of the school community. The report from the governors to the parents was brief and neutral, and there was an obvious initial nervousness. This rapidly disappeared and the atmosphere became animated. People felt free to raise whatever struck them as valuable and no one was afraid of voicing challenging opinions. There were cases of widely diverging attitudes but no bitterness. A full range of items was raised by parents: the new laws, sex education, tests, standards, craft design technology, computers, overspending, road safety, access to records, the role of the PTA.

The way ahead

Some dilemmas still remain unsolved. The timing of the governors' meetings at 4 pm is awkward for employed parents but ideal for those at home with young families. The representatives of ethnic-minority families are co-opted members and not elected parents. We need to explore the community's own perceptions as to how to overcome this. To involve more people it may be an idea for each class to have one or two parent representatives who meet regularly as a sub-committee and report to the parent governors before the full governing body meets, as a small school like us will still have only three parent governors after the new Act comes into force.

In spring 1985, Mary Martyn-Johns introduced a new system whereby instead of the head and staff submitting a separate report each, which is the usual pattern, we submit one school report, which we prepare at a staff meeting. This is not a ploy to silence the teachers' voice. It is a direct result of the head's vision of us all as a team. In future as parents are increasingly involved in school life, maybe one tripartite report will come into being from all of us concerned with the well-being of the school.

In short . . .

So far so good. The school distributes and displays letters and information from parent governors. Meetings are run democratically. Parent governors are centrally involved in all aspects of the business of the governing body and not simply relegated to less important areas of concern; parents know their elected representatives and are happy to talk to them about any matters which they want raising. The question of parent governors is not a contentious one at Redlands because general communication is good and because parents and staff see themselves as pursuing common goals rather than as potential adversaries.

This interpretation would seem to be borne out by attendance at the first annual parents' meeting with the governors. Ours was one of the very few meetings – local or national – which was quorate. The message seems self-evident: legislation alone will not cure all ills. It is impossible to get from A to Z in one move. Only by building solid and meaningful home-school links and by working towards open access can we expect parents to feel confident enough to make their views known to their elected representatives; to show their support by attending formal meetings; and to stand for election as governors themselves.

Parents' voices

Parents' views of parent governors . . .

- I like the idea of parent governors. If I had a problem with a child I'd go to the head; if there was a problem with the school, I'd go to the head and the parent governor. You feel you've got somebody else to go to if there's a problem. It helps in solving a problem if you can talk to as many different people as possible.
- When would I go to a parent governor? Well, I suppose I'd go about it in the same way I'd go about solving a problem at work. In the first instance I'd go to the ward sister, and only then would I go to a more senior nursing officer. If I had a problem with the school, first I would go to the class teacher. Then I would go to the head. Only if I didn't have satisfaction there would I take the issue up with a parent governor. I must say, though, that I've never needed to do that.
- In Redlands, the school makes a very positive effort to inform parents about policy and also makes a genuine attempt to take into consideration the views and wishes of parents. In such a school the importance of the parent governor may be less obvious than at schools which have suffered major conflicts of opinion between the school, teaching staff and governors.

The issues

- From the early days there was a sort of alliance of PTA parents and governors. We saw ourselves as a pressure group to support the head – especially regarding the LEA. We'd write to protest about staffing levels or plans for zoning secondary schools. We, above all people, had a vested interest in our own children's education.

- I was very worried about the sexism which you could see in many different aspects of the school. At one stage they actually had a beauty competition as part of a talent competition. I was appalled. I mentioned it to the previous head and while he said he agreed with me, he felt there were so many other things that needed to be done that this was a fairly low priority. I bided my time. With the election of a parent representative whom I knew would be prepared to take the issue on board, I thought it would be a good idea to get the matter discussed in general terms at a governors' meeting. It was actually more constructive to do it in this way than to start complaining about individual instances and individual teachers. It was well worth the effort. The issue was taken up as part of the staff's in-training sessions and there is now a policy document that I'm very satisfied with.
- As a governing body, we have had continuing battles with the county over extra staff to facilitate second language/mother tongue teaching and to accommodate the fact that our 'number of pupils registered' disguises the problems we face with a very heavy turnover of children. Bed and breakfast accommodation, the refuge, the fact that people move from two-bedroom houses near the school to larger homes out of the area when their first child comes to the end of the infant stage – all these mean that we have children in and out in large numbers, and this causes extra strain. Some children's unsettled homes mean extra strain re behaviour, too, and we try to get extra staff to compensate for that, e.g. assistants.
- As parent governor, I have been involved in the shortlisting and selection interview for the headteacher and now the deputy headteacher and I think that's an important role. We have, as parents, initiated discussion at governors' meetings on school meals, safety, transport to secondary school, sexism (in the sense of girls versus boys when behaviour is being judged, or when groups are chosen for an activity). I think most of these issues would not have been raised by the other governors because, except for the headteacher and the teacher rep., the relevance of them in our school would not have been known to them.

The meetings

- When the number of parent governors changed from one to two, we made a much stronger parent team.
- The meetings are preceded by a cup of tea with the teachers at 4 pm. At first this was very stilted, but conversation is becoming more animated. The meeting proper runs from 4.30 to 6.30ish. They are generally very good tempered affairs in spite of sharp political differences on occasion. I find it almost embarrassing sometimes to have the 'parent view' sought so assiduously. I can't imagine why I find it so, though, since we as families are the consumers!

Training

- The difficulty of having only one governors' meeting a term is that it takes a year or more to become familiar with the issues of staffing and finance that crop up and which are central all the time. The mysteries of Section 11, direct funding, capitation, advisers, etc. take time to unravel and this is where training is useful. I attended a series of evening meetings run as workshops by the National Association for Primary Education (NAPE) for the county council. There were about forty people taking part, some teacher reps, some local authority nominees, very few parents. The most useful parts were discussion with one of the county council's advisers on curriculum and a worksheet in groups – trying to decide what action we would/could take in a variety of situations, from noticing dry rot to taking part in a suspension/disciplinary meeting. I was surprised at how many members thought the proceedings of meetings were confidential; some of them had definitely been encouraged to think this by the chairman of their governing body. Many suggested a formality in their meetings which is almost entirely unkown in Redlands' governors' meetings.
- The Workers' Educational Association (WEA) occasionally runs a course, as does the Open University. In other words it is left up to the individual. Some basic training in the role of the school governor and the responsibilities of the governing body should be made more readily available to

governors. At this point I make no distinction between governors and parent governors because in the governing body there should be no difference.

Elections

- Why are people embarrassed by them? I'm sorry that many able people don't come forward – though, since the period of service is four years, there aren't, of course, many opportunities. Perhaps the infrequency of elections means that people don't get accustomed to the idea. On the other hand, since governors' meetings are held only three times a year, you do need to have several years' continuity of service.
- Any elections for the positions of parent governor should be as open as possible. There is a great temptation to avoid the ballot but I would like to see greater use of ballots. Unfortunately, not enough people have an adequate appreciation of what being a governor involves and therefore it often falls to parents already involved in other community activities. Sending out a letter asking for nominations is not enough; many more people would be prepared to put their name forward if they understood what was expected.
- For the first time since elections were introduced for parent governors, I really feel we're making progress. The number of people prepared to stand has always been very small, and they've usually had to have their arms twisted. With the vacancy that has just arisen, I've seen several groups of parents in deep conversation trying to decide on suitable nominees.

Representativeness

- It is important that parent governors should be the choice of parents, people that parents feel they can approach with trust and confidence. Parent governors should be prepared to represent the views of the general body of parents even when this does not coincide with their own personal view.
- I feel I am representative in the sense that I'm in school a great deal, talk to many parents in the playground and try to keep alert to what is concerning people. I think it would

be helpful if some of the Asian parents became interested
in serving as governors, but I don't think you should engineer
this just for the sake of getting someone to attend governors'
meetings. I'm sure the value of having a parent governor is
greater outside the meetings, in the sense that it needs to be
someone willing and able to chat to people round the school
and take part in the social events, etc., and therefore I'm in
favour of deliberately finding an Asian parent only if it's
someone willing to take on this role, i.e. I'm against
tokenism.

- I am in favour of positive encouragement of parents by parents
  – and there is an important difference between this and ballot
  rigging. This is one good way to ensure that a wide spectrum
  of parental views, backgrounds and ethnic origins is
  represented by the parent governors.

Reporting back

- I've not been as good at this as I should have been. I've
  usually put up an abbreviated summary of the meeting for
  people to read, but since the meetings centre very much on
  staff numbers; the need for more staff; requests for extra
  funding, etc., these are difficult to condense. I do talk to
  people I meet in the playground and try to follow up specific
  items, often through the PTA meetings.
- Reporting back to parents by parent governors tends to be
  done on an informal level. This is probably the most
  appropriate method where parent governors are readily
  accessible.
- The introduction of the new legal requirement for governing
  bodies to report annually to parents has added a new
  formality to what used to be passed on to parents by parent
  governors at the PTA AGM. The nature of this meeting will
  undoubtedly vary from school to school, depending on the
  nature of the relationship between the school and the
  parents, the school and the governing body, and the
  effectiveness of the parent governors.

Children's voices

- Mums and Dads who were already in the school chose my mum. They wanted her as one of the school governors. I think they chose her because they liked her. They must have been confident that she was the best person.
- I hope the governors can help us get more things. I've nearly finished the maths cards and I think I'll need a book next.
- It's nice that my mother is a parent governor. When she's at meetings I get the choice of whether to go to our nextdoor neighbour's or somewhere else, so I have more time to spend with my friends.
- I expect my mum enjoys the meetings and I don't mind her going as long as I can play with Dominic.
- It's mainly about telling the other governors what school is about and the work they are doing.
- My mum wanted to be a governor because she likes helping the children in the school.
- It's a good idea to have parents as governors because they know better than the other governors what their children are doing in school and they can make comments on it.
- When my dad was chairman of the governors – and the PTA – it was like being a postman. 'Oh! not another letter to take home,' I'd think.

Chapter 9

Parents as helpers

The activities of PTAs, more open access to school and better channels of communication with parents, the appointment of parent governors – all these things helped to break down the 'them and us' mentality so prevalent for so long and made it possible for a new kind of parent involvement. Ever since the mid-seventies increasing numbers of parents have been coming into school as classroom helpers. This development is by no means without its critics, since it coincided with an increase in educational cuts. Yet moral scruples about parents working alongside teachers as unpaid aides can be looked at from another perspective. Parents identify a wide range of benefits both for themselves and their children and are seldom, if ever, unwilling to take part in this kind of venture.

At Redlands, we felt we had a firm foundation to build on: the PTA was working well; our communications with parents were good; there was now a tradition of parents coming into school to see the fruits of our labours and to applaud their children's progress. We wanted to capitalize on the obvious interest which people were showing. It was all very well to create a new library, to insist that books be kept in a good state of repair, that all new books be covered . . . but, at a time when staffing cuts were just starting and pressures on teachers were mounting, who was to do all this? The obvious answer seemed to be . . . parents.

Last term, a student teacher said to me, 'I think parents are just used in most schools'. Being useful, needed by someone, for something, seems to me to be what keeps most of us sane. However, I knew from her tone and the stress she afforded the word 'used' that she meant something unflattering. She was implying that parents were used as skivvies and not respected or valued by schools. I do hope she is wrong.

In the case of Redlands, I can say with honesty that we looked to parents for help in those early days as you would look to friends. We felt they would recognize that we needed support, that we would be grateful for any help they could give, and that we would understand if none was forthcoming. It did not seem unfair to ask parents to work alongside teachers, to take pride in the new library, to help with cataloguing, to cover books and so on.

Not always a bed of roses

As with most walks of life, there are dreary facets to teaching as well as fascinating ones and there are numerous boring but essential tasks to be undertaken if a school is to be run smoothly and efficiently. Vast amounts of art paper have to be cut, paints have to be mixed, display boards have to be backed, children's pictures have to be mounted . . . all of which takes hours. I remember only too vividly when I changed from secondary to primary teaching and had to do this for the first time. I was staggered at how long it took! So, operating as a teacher's aide may not be glamorous but it is worth its weight in gold.

Lego and all the other plastic construction equipment that you find in abundance in almost any primary classroom has to be washed and disinfected at the end of each term. Children's trays and drawers need the same treatment. Paint overalls and dressing-up clothes need washing too and occasionally repairing. For years, like many teachers, I imagine, I did all that myself during the holidays. It never occurred to me to look to anyone else to give me a hand. Now, with the help of parents, we get through it all in a day. One inventive mother tipped all the Lego into a pillow-case to take home to do in her washing machine. What used to be a tedious chore has turned into a social event as we nudge each other out of the way to get to the sink or complain about the dearth of dry teatowels!

The other side of the coin

If it were only the boring, messy jobs that were handed over to parents or if teachers were not prepared to get their hands dirty too then, yes, I would think it unfair and parents (or student teachers on their behalf) would have every right to object. But there are myriad other more interesting and creative jobs to be done around a school.

Mounting and displaying children's work is one example. Another is running the school bookshop after school. I was not surprised that parents were keen to take this on. I had certainly found it a rewarding job so I assumed others might well find it so. It is an interesting way of keeping abreast of new titles and authors and children's taste and some parents were every bit as eager as I was to do just that.

There are plenty of more sociable activities than the solitary task of mixing paints. Decorating the playground with streamers and lights, the hall with Christmas decorations, making games for the Summer Fair – all these move us into areas that are likely to be more fun, if only because they usually involve a group working together. Parents' motives for coming into school are mixed, no doubt, and as well as wishing to see what is going on and to be a part of that, some may well seek company and companionship.

Teachers need to be perceptive about individual parents' sensitivities. Many of the tasks I have mentioned could be done outside the classroom and diffident parents may well prefer it that way, to begin with at least. For other parents, this kind of exclusion may increase a feeling of isolation or being taken for granted and an invitation to work inside rather than outside the classroom may well be overdue.

Blinkered vision

For a long time when we are planning special celebrations we have asked parents to sign up on the board in the entrance hall to say what sort of food will be contributed and then to bring it along on the appointed day. I am sure many schools will recognize this system of ensuring enough variety on the day. I wonder how many parents are then asked to stay on to soak up the party atmosphere and to have the pleasure of seeing their own children enjoying themselves in school? All too often it is the chosen few who are honoured with an invitation to stay. Even then, is it only to see to the food and the washing up? Or can they come into the hall with the teachers and join in the party games?

I still feel ashamed of myself as I write this, having been caught without realizing it in this trap for many years. I, too, had always asked specific parents to help. It had always been like that and I did not think to question it at first. Yet an open invitation is much better, for all the obvious reasons. In my experience numbers have never been a problem as not every parent is free and many do not relish the idea of fun and games with a hundred five- to seven-year-olds.

There was always a sea of faces at the glass pannelled door watching teachers and children playing the party games. I recall the first time one brave mother opened the door and came in to join us. I felt a distinct pang of annoyance that she had over-stepped the mark and wandered from her accepted role as tea lady. My instinctive reaction appalled me! Seconds later as the door opened again and other parents followed her example, I realized how absurd my initial feelings had been and recovered in time to smile and beckon them in. Since then the atmosphere at school parties has been much more spontaneous.

Out and about

Probably the most exhausting task is helping out on school trips, whether to the local library, to the Festival Hall for children's concerts, to museums or on summer outings. The success of these events depends upon the preparation and organization before-hand. If parents know exactly which children will be in their group, what the order of procedure is, what the aim of the outing is and how we hope to achieve it, then there is far less chance of accidents and much more chance that everyone will have an enjoyable day. In fact, recent Health and Safety rules make parental support an absolute must for a relatively small primary school such as Redlands whenever we leave the premises with a class of children to go to the swimming pool or the sports field each week, or to the local shops as part of a project.

Coming into their own

When falling rolls meant a classroom became free, we converted it to a cookery room. For a teacher to do cookery with a whole class of primary school children is not at all practical. It is an activity which is best done in small groups. Waiting for your turn to have the one and only general assistant would have meant that children hardly ever got to do cooking. This obvious area of need paved the way for parents to get a foothold on activities with more status.

We started by approaching parents that we knew to be free to make a regular commitment. We felt that continuity was an important factor, especially for the younger children. Working on the assumption that the better you know the children the more you enjoy working with them, we also thought that continuity would be important for the parents.

For some time it was left entirely to the teachers to decide about recipes and to organize the buying of ingredients. Gradually, parents came across interesting recipes or old favourites that they wanted to share with their groups. They have gone on to share with the teacher the planning of the term's work or, indeed, in some cases, to take full responsibility for the term's sessions to fit in with the theme being studied. Thus, for the first time for our school, parents had a direct influence over one area of the curriculum. Only a handful of parents, I admit, but it was a start.

There were the expected difficulties. Because of daily contact, infant classes found it easier to recruit volunteers. It is largely mothers that are free to undertake cooking sessions, although we have involved three or four men in recent years. Added to that, by the time their children have reached the junior stage, many women decide to take a full-time or a part-time job again so cannot make a weekly commitment to the school. Some feel disinclined to take on a group of pre-adolescents. Yet, one way or another, we have always managed to staff cookery sessions for all classes, an achievement which would have been totally impossible without parents.

Craft is another area that I, for one, have been very glad to have expert help with. Sewing buttons back on was my absolute zenith with a needle, and because of my own shortcomings in this area I feel future generations of men and women should at least have a basic knowledge of sewing. After discussions about aims for the term and talents of particular children, I have been able to hand over decisions to parents about which materials to order, what crafts to teach, what garments to attempt. I have learned much about weaving, macramé, knitting, embroidery, tie-dying, and Rajasthani mirror work, not to mention more basic sewing skills and have rejoiced in the delight and pride of the children with waistcoats, kimonos, and skirts that they have dyed and stitched themselves.

It was not a big step from being responsible for specific tasks to becoming involved in general work in the art area. It crept in first when we were undertaking a major project, working co-operatively with the head, Mike Richards, and a couple of parents. The children rotated round the four of us, for instance, for the sequence of operations in silk screen printing, or for designing and printing Christmas cards and wrapping paper. Occasionally, the whole class works together on a project in this way but, more often, a parent, or school governor even, volunteers to make a regular commitment to the art work. Being available for the art area does not mean merely mixing paints, preparing mounds of paper, keeping the table tidy, and clearing up afterwards. It also involves serious discussion with individual children or a small group of children about choice of materials and tools, about technique, effects, colour choice, shapes, evaluation of results and suggestions for future work. Once parents realized the educational potential, there was much greater willingness to be involved in art work.

The way we respond to children's work is vitally important. It seems to me to be a crucial factor in a child's experience in school. I feel it is essential that we show children that we are interested in whatever they do, that we care enough to discuss the work while in progress and on completion, and are available to guide tactfully without destroying confidence. I love being involved in that way with children. There is plenty of research evidence which shows that parents do, too, at home – so why not at school?

We assumed that some parents would be interested in engaging reception age children in conversation and thus help develop their language along the lines of Joan Tough's work in the seventies,[1] which was in vogue at that time. So in the early eighties, by invitation again, mothers were asked to devote a session to playing alongside the new starters in the home corner, or to join a group on the carpeted area building Lego models, very much in the way a general assistant might have been employed to foster language development at the pre-reading stage. Hand in hand with that went tasks for the pre-numeracy stage, playing games to reinforce colour recognition or classification techniques, then graduating to early work on weighing and capacity. It was still very much the preserve of the chosen few and with the underlying feeling of compensatory education. But at least it was a move towards parental involvement in the core-curriculum area.

Some dilemmas

There is no denying that it is mostly women who are free to help during school hours in our area. If we look again at the list of jobs I have been talking about – preparation, washing, cooking, serving – they fit all too neatly into the stereotypical role of women, which the school might well be working towards altering. Over the last five years, a few fathers have run cookery classes and occasionally men have been free to help at parties and to go on outings but I have not had one turning up for the grand end of term cleaning routine – yet! We intend to keep looking for every opportunity to provide children with a wide range of different roles for both women and men.

We were also anxious about how best to approach parent helpers. We debated whether to wait until parents volunteered or whether to approach them directly; whether all parents felt welcome and at ease; whether some felt pressurized and guilty if they did not contribute; whether to put up notices for willing parents to sign (but what about illiterate parents or parents who were not literate in English, or parents who did not regularly fetch their children and would therefore never see the notices?); whether to specify the jobs required by the teacher and run the risk of missing something the teacher might not have thought of, thus letting valuable expertise go to waste. In the end none of these problems proved insurmountable and at some point we tried all the various ways of going about things. As long as people felt relaxed together and eager to get on with the job in hand, the details seemed to take care of themselves.

Parents as experts

As time went by and the staff began to knit together as a unit, the idea of termly themes for the whole school sprang up. Then efforts were made to seek out those parents who were experts in the appropriate fields – paper-making, building, Kenya, spices for making tea the Indian way and so on. If we heard of something that would fit our interests that term, such as making Russian tea, boys' and girls' day in Japan, or Carnival in Trinidad, we ventured beyond parents at times to invite teachers from neighbouring schools, lecturers from the university and members of the local community.

Since many of Redlands' children attend other educational establishments outside the formal school day, staff visited the Koran school at the mosque and the Punjabi school at the Gudwara to show support and further our knowledge. We also supported community initiatives such as the Bengali Saraswati Puja and the Indian Workers' Association events. In all of these activities our language support teacher played a major part, spending a great deal of time on home visits and meals with families. As ever, there are no losers: everyone involved has benefited.

Celebrations associated with Christmas spread to Diwali and Eid. Older sisters and mothers come in and demonstrate a wide range of skills to the children: they decorate hands with mendhi patterns, make burfi and other sweetmeats and tell the traditional stories behind the festivals. All of this has become an integral part of accepted school traditions, not a tokenistic or exotic extra.

Bilingual parents have contributed in many other ways, too: helping build up a bank of taped stories in the mother tongue; making a collection of lullabies from their own childhood; telling stories in their mother tongue; choosing artefacts and clothing for the home corner. In 1986 one of our Pakistani mothers was appointed as a part-time mother tongue teacher in Redlands and, since 1981, the wife of one of our governors has been teaching an Urdu class for any interested juniors in school time.

The present head, Mary Martyn-Johns, has opened the door of the hall as well as the classroom to parents. She has invited a variety of speakers into our assemblies: a grandmother demonstrating her lacemaking skills, a husband showing his antique camera and a mother demonstrating how to make a proper curry. As parents saw how they were valued and what a crucial role they played in the life of the school, they became less inhibited about offering their special skills. It became a much more frequent occurrence to bump into parents around the school.

Once we started extending the range of clubs run by teachers at lunchtime and after school, parents were quick to come forward, so that now the bookshop, the chess club, recorder, computer, football, netball and badminton clubs are all entirely organized and managed by parents. It has not always been easy for them. Sometimes, for instance, it has meant liaising with kitchen staff and dinner controllers to alter times of lunches. The present head is meticulous in ensuring that everybody's job descriptions are spelled out, that everything is talked through in advance, that everyone's suggestions are encouraged, that people are then trusted to get on with their jobs.

On the brink

There was no shortage of parental involvement in school, yet we still had a nagging feeling that most of the parents' work was on the periphery of the curriculum and to a large extent the core curriculum was in the hands of the professionals. We had flirted in the early eighties with involving parents with the teaching of reading, by inviting two mothers – of impeccable academic pedigree! – to work in a withdrawal situation on the Tasmanian project. This was a scheme that was much publicized as the time, involving taping individual children's favourite stories for them to listen to at leisure. It is interesting to note that the two junior boys chosen to take part in the project were both having problems with their reading, a common starting-point for parental involvement in the teaching of reading.

In 1986 I heard Joan Sallis, then chairperson of CASE, talking about the odd position schools take up, allowing parents to cover various areas of the curriculum other than the basics without realizing they are giving out strong messages about how they rate those other areas. The hidden curriculum at work with a vengeance! I thought back to those early days at Redlands when we were indeed guilty of that very thing. It was some time before we added reading to the list of tasks that parents might like to be involved in.

At first, few parents volunteered, which is not altogether surprising in a school which had built up such a mystique about reading. The parents who did become involved soon spread the word and there was no further shortage of volunteers.

I arranged a meeting with parents interested in helping with reading to discuss ideas. I did this not because I thought mine was the only way to set about the task, but because by then the school had an agreed policy on language intended to ensure a common approach throughout a child's school life. For the sake of continuity, it seemed sensible for the parents helping in class to use the same approach as the teachers.

We discussed the organization of the sessions, strategies we hoped to encourage in the readers, and strategies that had proved successful for the adult listeners to use when a child was stuck. I did feel wary at first and I remember handing over to parents only the more experienced readers and keeping the beginners to myself! Strange when you consider that at junior level I had channelled the two boys experiencing difficulties towards parents.

In short

The value of having more than one adult in the classroom is inestimable. Even in an ideal world with smaller classes and low pupil-teacher ratios, parents would still have a valuable part to play. Parent helpers make an enormous difference to the quality of education we offer in schools. They like learning more about the curriculum at first hand, they enjoy the involvement with their own and other people's children, they appreciate the social aspects of working in school. Children, for their part, make no bones about the pleasure they derive from seeing their parents in school.

Teachers, too, have learned a lot. We have moved a long way from the time when we thought that only 'educated' parents should be allowed to help in the classroom. It took me a long time as a teacher to trust children to be responsible for their own learning, and even longer to realize that trusting parents to do a good job worked every bit as well. We have ended up with all concerned feeling part of the team and proud of what is being achieved. There is a valuable knock-on effect too. The way that adults treat each other in school stands as an example for how children will treat each other and this affects the whole atmosphere of the school.⟩

Parents' voices

Reasons for helping . . .

- I got roped in to do the cooking. I didn't have the nerve to say no! I did it for a term and I thoroughly enjoyed it once I was there.
- When the last child leaves home to start school some parents feel as if they are not needed any more during the day, but if these parents are welcomed into the school they can still feel part of their children's education. The parent can be made to feel an outcast in some schools, but the schools that are friendly and welcoming usually have willing helpful people to do the jobs that are extra to the school timetable.
- I appreciate being asked to help with groups of children – it is lovely to meet the girls' friends in this way. I feel very honoured that we are allowed to use the staff-room – do the staff feel the lack of privacy? Where do they go for a good gripe?
- I like working with the children. It doesn't matter whose children they are.
- I'm learning all the time. My confidence has grown. I used to jump if you said, 'Boo!'
- You get involved. You are contributing. You feel you have achieved something – you've helped the children learn something they didn't know.
- I wonder sometimes about whether we are doing work which would actually be done by teachers if it wasn't for the educational cutbacks. But, quite frankly, I'm not prepared to sit back on a point of principle and let my children miss out on the benefits of having extra adults in the classroom. Besides, I actually enjoy being in school and my children really like me to be involved, too.
- I like working with a group of children. It's quite different from working with your own child. You don't get ratty when they don't understand.

- I sometimes wonder what it would be like to be bored. If Redlands fell down I might find out but I expect the staff would start a rebuilding project needing parents' help!

Different activities . . .

- It's not like some schools I know where it's like being in the army and you have a rota for parents for jobs like tidying up, washing the paint brushes, mopping the floor, and the teachers don't do anything.

Cooking and sewing . . .

- My daughter came home and announced that each class wanted volunteers, one for sewing, one for cooking. I think I was a bit worried at first – I wondered what I'd let myself in for. We decided they could make aprons and use them for their cooking! It was the first stages, so there was a bit of a feeling of 'That's girls' stuff' from the odd couple of boys. The teacher gave in to them and they got out of it. I'll never forget that! Apart from those few, the children were ever so friendly and I got to know them all. I used to take my younger daughter with me. She was tiny and terribly shy. I'm sure it helped her to be with all those children. They loved her and used to make such a fuss of her.
- I thoroughly enjoy doing the cooking when only one group comes in the afternoon. Then they can do it all themselves and there's time for a lovely conversation with them. Otherwise it's like a conveyor belt with you rushing through the whole class, just being the person who throws the ingredients in really. But with one group, I feel they know me as a person. They come up and talk to me in the street and are all excited about doing cookery with me.
- I enjoy doing cooking. I'm very organized and I like being in charge. You feel they've learned something. They have to measure everything and know exactly how they made it. I decide what we'll cook – sometimes it's connected with the topic they're doing. Sometimes I wish the teacher had some suggestions!
- I'm sure some parents believe that coming in to do cooking

is hard work, but it's not. The children actually do all the cooking themselves. I didn't believe this when my son would bring things home, but I've seen for myself now and they actually do.

- I help with the cooking because I'd hate for them not to learn how to cook and somebody has to do it. If you're not careful you could end up doing it 2 or 3 times a week.
- My daughter has definitely appreciated the extra attention she gets in the small groups parents take out for cooking and sewing. Personally, I am hopeless at the latter and she loves it. Perhaps small groups could get out of the school more often?
- I get carried away doing the sewing. I forget where I am. It's not like being in school. I have real conversations with the children. They're so friendly and we really get to know each other.
- I offered to do cooking and sewing. It was my own decision. I could cope with them. There were loads of other things I could do – computer, typing, writing – but I felt happier with the cooking and sewing.
- I like being in the class with my sewing group. You can listen to what's going on. It's quite funny at times.

Sport

- I especially enjoyed doing the badminton after school and going to the field with the juniors. My son said they wouldn't be able to go to the field if I didn't help. I had a group. The kids thoroughly enjoyed it. It was good having a mum playing football and getting away from traditional roles.

School trips . . .

- Because, like most fathers, I can't make a regular commitment to helping in the classroom, I try to make time to go on trips. It's fun. It helps you get to know the other children in your own child's class. It's a very useful reminder of the task that faces the teacher. When you sigh with relief at the end of the day because *you* don't have to go back into school the next day, it really makes you appreciate the teacher.

- I don't necessarily spend all or even most of the time with my own child on trips, but it's very important for him to know that I'm there. It also helps me build up a better picture of what's going on in the class – both in terms of group dynamics and the kind of work they are doing. We recently went to the library to look at street lists and find out who had lived in our houses before we had. It was fascinating.

Being an expert . . .

- I enjoyed coming in to talk to the kids about Kenya. I think lots of parents would like it. Instead of having just teas with cakes and Eid or Diwali parties all the time, I'd say it would be better to tell parents a specific time on such and such a day, that's your time to come in and talk to the class about anything that interests you – it's your choice. A regular thing: parents sharing with the kids.
- For the publishing project, there was no shortage of parent experts to call on. One of the parents knows how to make paper; because of the links with the university, several have written books; there's a copy editor and some graphic artists. It would have been stupid not to involve us in what was going on. My greatest moment was when one of the children in my son's class asked if she could interview me!

Feeling at home . . .

- At our last school it was 'You're quite welcome but you will leave the little ones at home, won't you?' So, of course, you never bothered going in. At Redlands when I did the cooking, the little one went and played with the Lego.
- I don't think you appreciate it fully until your children go to secondary school. I've no idea what they do there.
- There's a lovely atmosphere in the nursery. You can have a good role play with the kids – wonderful for the imagination. Or you can play games, read stories, go out for a walk. It's open door and you feel you can go in whenever you like. You get to know all the other children and the parents. And it spreads outside the school. It's a community and you watch out for each other's children.

- As a parent who has worked in the school for nearly six years now I feel part of a friendly, growing team. People have come and gone but the happy atmosphere of the school has developed. Redlands without parents would be like an empty beehive. It seems to buzz with activity from staff, parents and children.
- It's really nice to be able to go in and help. You're welcome at any time.

Children's Voices

Feelings on parents as helpers . . .

- It's extra special having my mum to help in our class.
- Mummy's good at helping. She helped all my friends as well.
- I like parents helping in the class. They don't nag you as much as teachers do.
- I didn't want my dad to go. I wanted him to stay all day. I'd like to help in school when I'm a mummy, but not all day . . . only if I could afford the time.

Why parents help . . .

- Some people get quite lonely when they're new, or if you've just come from a long way away. Like, we've got a new girl in our class and she can't speak English yet. It would help her a lot if her mum came in, wouldn't it?
- The teachers don't have enough time and I reckon they probably need a helping hand around the classroom. Andrew's mum stuck the times tables on card. I reckon it does help you learn.
- It's a good thing. The teachers don't have enough time to go round everybody. If there are parents in the class, it's easier.
- When parents come into the school it's good because they know what school is like for you.

Cooking and sewing . . .

- My mum's good at cooking. She made nice things with my class like biscuits and little cakes and jam tarts.
- My dad's at home now so my mum can come to school. I like her to do just cooking, because that's what I like.
- Tommy's mum is good for cooking. She helps us and she's very good at it. She's always got good recipes.
- Will somebody still be doing sewing? I'd like to see if somebody's parent could come in and I thought we could make puppets. We have made puppets before, but I mean proper ones that work.
- Some mums don't work and they don't want to hang around the house all day so they can come in and do some cooking with us.

Reading . . .

- My Mum does the bookshop every Friday. I like that because I can read the books or I can play in the playground. She buys me a book sometimes. Sometimes I buy one with my own money.
- I liked my mum reading with me best of all.
- My mum comes every Friday to help us read.

Clubs

- My dad did two clubs – computer and chess. He used to bring me for afternoon nursery so on club days I had my dinner in the hall.

Outings . . .

- We went to a farm. There were a lot of insects. We fed some animals and you could climb in with the rabbits and have a stroke. My mum came to help with my group. She nearly lost somebody. He went in with the goats and that wasn't allowed and he got knocked around. My mum was cross and at the end she was tired.
- When you go on trips, if there are parents you can have more groups and smaller groups.

- When my dad comes on school trips he's very good at thinking up games and competitions to keep us busy.

Parents as experts . . .

- It was really good when my mum and dad brought our puppies into school.
- Someone had found some old lace bobbins, so I asked my granny to come to assembly to tell the whole school about how she did lace. She did some demonstrating in assembly because she was staying with us for a while. People said they were really pleased with my granny. That was the first time I'd ever, ever seen a bit of demonstrating done by somebody not from the school. It's coming into my mind that gramps could do his woodworking. You'd need dirty mats to catch all the woodshaving though . . .
- My dad has been in to talk about Africa. Look – the girls remember, they're smiling. We all asked some questions – Daddy didn't know some of the answers.

Helping at home . . .

- While you're in the holidays you don't have to have a rest from school, you can still go on learning. You could get a hard book from the library and do a page or two with your mummy or daddy and afterwards you can try it by yourself. That's a good way of learning.
- When it's Saturday and Sunday we practise what my dad thinks I'm not very good at – like sums. Best of all, I like tens and units. My dad draws the sums and I just do it.
- My teacher said I'm not very good at maths, but I'm getting better now because my mum's helping me. We do the numbers in Japanese at home.
- At home my dad gives me handwriting and maths and I do them all.

Chapter 10

Parents' mornings

Like schools elsewhere, Redlands has witnessed the shift from parents doing only the more menial tasks like repairing and clearing up to taking on responsibility for activities like cooking and sewing, to helping with reading. We have also witnessed the demise of the myth that parents have to be highly educated before they can be considered an asset in the classroom. Of course, the closer to the core curriculum, the more controversial parent participation becomes, because it challenges the role of the teacher as expert. Yet, more and more, educational research into effective classroom practice has been pointing not to the teacher as expert, but to the teacher as facilitator with children as active partners in their own learning. There has also been a mass of evidence from Dagenham, Haringey and Coventry – to name but a few – which has proved that parental involvement in reading is very effective. Some of us began to ask ourselves – why stop at reading?

I suppose we had reached a watershed at Redlands by 1985, with things ticking over nicely but with a persistent feeling that something was lacking. We did not know it at the time, but a solution was in sight. One of the tiresome chores of being a deputy head is sifting through all the mail, masses of which arrives daily. The pessimist's view of the situation! One of the perks of being a deputy head is that you have first look at all the mail, including the envelope full of the in-service courses on offer for the term. The optimist's view of the situation! I am an optimist. One particular batch of letters yielded an item about a one-day course at the University of Reading on parental involvement in the classroom. A definite must.

On the day, two teachers from Foxhill School, Sheffield recounted their experiences of organizing parents' workshops of a rather special kind. Parents came into school to work with their own child for an hour or so one morning a week on a regular basis. I grasped straight away by their tone that their attitude towards parents was very similar to ours: a firm commitment to parents' right to be involved in their children's education, a firm belief in parents' genuine interest in their children's education, a firm belief in parents' ability as educators in their own right.

As I listened, it dawned on me that the situation of parents in their school prior to the launching of the project in 1981 was very similar to the one we enjoyed at Redlands – parents on committees as fund-raisers, parents as governors, as dinner controllers, as escorts on school trips, as organizers of clubs, as classroom helpers.

Although half of my mind carried on listening to the speakers and my pen went on making notes of all the details, the other half of my mind was already leaping ahead envisaging how we could put a similar scheme into action at Redlands, where the employment situation was different, where the ethnic mix was different, where the emphasis in the teaching of reading was different. None of that seemed to matter: the seed was sown. I knew it could work.

Back home, at the end of the day, I phoned Mary Martyn-Johns to pass on the news. I knew that I could rely on her giving the idea a fair hearing, a thorough critical appraisal, and a positive response if she felt it to be educationally valid. We closeted ourselves in her office the next day after school, to go over the details. We pored over the Foxhill set-up itself; we discussed individual parents and the likelihood of their being free in the mornings; we talked about one-parent families, parents who were both employed, full- or part-time; we went over my timetable to find the most convenient morning from the school's point of view; we looked carefully at the list of children in my class in case we felt such a project might prove detrimental to any child if their parent was unable to take part; we questioned whether any of the new starters would be unsettled again by seeing their parents come and go in this way; we pondered about parents with limited English and perhaps no reading ability in English. (We always tried to promote the use of mother tongue in the classroom, but we wondered if it would worry the parents if they were seen to be unable to read along with their child a text written in English.) All in all, some reservations but even so, we were both very excited by the idea and felt it was worth a try.

It was decided that I would act as guinea pig for the first term at least. If it proved to be a flop there would be no harm done as I had been a teacher long enough not to feel a total failure when things did not work out as hoped. If, on the other hand, the project proved successful, then we could consider extending it to other classes.

Having taught at the school for several years, I felt I had built up good relationships with the parents of my pupils. My classroom offered open access to parents in the morning, at lunch time and after school, when work done by the children could be shown to parents and friends. I did this partly so that I was not the only audience for a child's work, and partly so that parents could share instantly in the successes as they arose day by day. I imagined that the parents, too, were ready to break new ground.

The following morning as I greeted them, I told them in brief about the course I had just been on, and how I thought we could tackle such a scheme together. I left the grapevine to operate, to give them some time to think about it on their own, without any pressure from the school. I am not good at hiding my feelings though, so I expect my enthusiasm was evident. By the end of the week, letters had gone out to all of the parents concerned and we were ready to go.

On the appointed morning, the head took my class, and I gathered the parents in the school library for a cup of tea and a chat. With hindsight, it was not a good place to have chosen as so many people turned up that we were far too squashed. I had also been unable to arrange for our interpreter to be present, as the meeting had been arranged so quickly. If I had the time over again, I would have arranged the meeting to fit the interpreter's availability. First impressions are so important when introducing something new and clarity is essential if you want to avoid anxiety.

I then explained the project to them. There was no doubt about their interest. Of course, there were questions raised and wrinkles to be ironed out. I pointed out, for instance, that it was not necessary to speak fluent Queen's English to be able to help one's child. It was just as valuable to talk to children about books in their first language . . . and we had quite a selection of first languages: Urdu, Panjabi, Farsi, Arabic, Spanish and French.

I could tell that the idea of a regular commitment worried some people. What would happen if they could not make it every week? Would their child suffer? Could they bring younger siblings along? Yes, of course – there were plenty of attractions to keep them busy. One mother, soon to have a baby, realized that it would be some time before she could be free to join in. Her daughter's best friend's father offered to be a substitute parent in the meantime and take on a twosome. I jumped in quickly to point out that that would not be unusual. We operated a vertically grouped system in the Infants and several families had two children in my class. Thus a parent with a child tucked in on either side would be quite normal. In fact, this aspect pleased me as I believe strongly in co-operative learning.

In the event, pram and newborn baby became standard features in the classroom. So did breast-feeding. Parents who had recently separated decided to take turns, week in week out, so that both could share in their child's learning, which I thought was an ideal solution to a tricky situation. One family with both parents working, opted to send a trusted friend along as a substitute, and grandparents and older siblings with time to spare were welcome as a matter of course.

First steps

We arranged to meet the following Thursday to run through a programme for the term. We changed the venue as we had been so cramped the previous week. The only space big enough was the hall, which was used for assemblies, dinners and PE sessions, which meant that one class would have to forgo its gym lesson that morning. Not ideal, but then compromises are often necessary in the real world. As in the previous week, the head took my class and parents and I gathered in the hall as soon as the children were settled in class. During the week I had drawn up a rough plan of how I saw these sessions working out. I thought we would concentrate on reading to start with and have half an hour sharing books together and the other half an hour as a library session, with two groups doing each activity at a time so we would not be too crowded either in the classroom or in the library.

I began the session by recapping the gist of our new parents' meetings to reinforce our beliefs about the way children learn to read and how we aim to help them become fluent, silent readers. Together we mulled over my handout, and I explained if, when and how to react when children miscue, emphasizing that reading is an active, thinking process that involves taking risks. I answered any questions as they arose.

I had brought into the hall a selection of boxes of books. Then we went into a role-play exercise where I played the parent/teacher role and one of the parents, whom I knew could handle the situation, played the part of a child and we acted out a typical reading session together. We read books from various levels, making links with the stages that individual children from the class were at, since obviously, one's tactics as adult-listener vary according to whether the child is brand new to the printed word, whether the child has some sight vocabulary or whether the child is making rapid progress towards internalization.

We spent a long time after this on specific examples that parents cited from their own experiences with their own children till we all felt that we knew where we were heading with children and books. Then we moved on to consider what we might do in the library session. I pointed out Berkshire's system for colour coding non-fiction books which was in use in our school library. As I started to tell everyone how I normally handled the library lesson, I could see brows puckering, frantic glances darting to and fro. I sensed that they were not able to form a clear picture from my description! It was not difficult for me as I had been doing it for some time and so I had a clear mental image as I talked. This was not the case for the parents, trying to cope in the abstract with a totally new idea. Playtime was approaching . . . saved by the bell, you might say. But it was important to finish on a positive note, not in confusion, so we came to the decision that the following week I would take my normal library session, with the parents as observers, and they could fit the theory to the practice on the spot.

Up to this point, I had been concentrating fully on parents and had forgotten the children! Fortunately, a parent pointed out that the children had not realized it was to be another talking morning for parents and they were expecting them in the classroom. I was mortified not to have picked that up myself, but delighted that parents had pointed this out. We just had time for a quick cuddle and a peep at the morning's work before the children went out to play and those parents who were free joined us in the staff-room for tea or coffee.

Thursday, 12 February 1985

The first real parents' morning dawned. I was very excited but I had not anticipated the enthusiasm of the children nor the nervousness of some of the parents. Usually parents breezed into the classroom looking at Lego models, paintings, stories, maths or whatever their own child was keen for them to see. Some did just that this particular morning, too, taking off their coats and carrying on as normal. One or two others sat and chatted to each other, muttering in disbelief at how uncomfortable the tiny infant chairs were. Some, to my surprise, hovered at the door, fingering coat buttons, unsure of whether or not to take their coats off, where to go exactly, whether to stay standing or sit down.

Registration was fairly noisy. Children were beaming, waving to their mums and dads and telling their friends to do likewise. The parents were by then all talking fifty to the dozen to each other. I took it as a compliment that they were so quickly their normal selves again and did not feel that they had to sit with their arms folded and backs straight in stony silence! Confession time. On some occasions in the weeks that followed, I felt slightly irritated by this loud background chatter of the parents while I was trying to discuss something with the children but I knew the parents well enough to be honest, turn round and say, 'Come on, folks, you're making so much noise, we can't hear ourselves think over here.' Or 'I don't know what we are going to do with your mums and dads, they aren't listening, are they?' in a tone that I hope no one found offensive.

I was torn in those early days between (a) feeling that the parents needed some social time together and valued those five minutes while I talked to the children; (b) wondering whether it was a bad example for the children to see their parents talking while I was talking, and (c) hoping that the parents would want to listen to what the children and I had to say. I need not have worried as the problem solved itself as time went by. Gradually parents crept nearer to the carpeted area and began to join in the initial daily discussion with the children. The carpeted area was rather small so there was no question of parents joining children even if they had all been prepared to squat on the floor. It seems incredible to me now that I took a year to think of moving to the other side of the carpet so that the audience I faced included parents as well as children!

Upstairs to the library we went, clutching the pile of books returned from last week. Children and parents browsed together and chose the books they wanted to take home. I showed parents how I would help a child to find his or her card, in alphabetical order by surname in the file, write in this week's chosen title, cross out last week's if returned. Also how to help children to return their books to the correct shelf, using the colour-coded system, set out on a poster on the wall; how to ensure that the children put the book the right way up, the right way round and how to make a space for it on the shelf without forcing it in and thereby crumpling all the pages . . . all the things that an adult takes for granted but that children have to learn.

There was time for looking at books together, perhaps to read a story or some poems, perhaps to read the work displayed round the walls, perhaps to talk about the artefacts supplied on loan from the Schools Museum Service. When everyone's book choice had been recorded, then we gathered together for a joint teaching session. Right from the beginning, I start the process of guiding children towards becoming independent learners and one of my main targets is the library and how to find one's way around it. A few quick quiz questions, as a bit of fun, to start us off.

T: Where would I find a large picture book?
C1: [Points].
T: Brilliant. What if I want a story book, a longer one with chapters?
C2: Over there
T: Fantastic. Now, what about a poetry book?
C2: That shelf there.
T: How do we recognize poetry books?
C2: They've got black and red stickers.

Over the weeks, we go through in turn each colour section, starting with the ones that seem most popular with most children and leaving until last the less used categories, the ones which are more difficult for children to identify as categories at all. I often start with dark green, things that grow.

> T: Ceri wants to find a book about sharks. Can anyone help him?
>
> C3: In dark green.
>
> T: Let's try that then . . . (while he's looking) What else would we find in dark green, do you think?
>
> C4: Animals.
>
> C5: Plants.
>
> C6: Birds.
>
> C7: Insects.
>
> C8: Elephants.
>
> T: What about people? Will they be in there?
>
> And so on.

We check through the books in each section to make sure we know about everything we can find there. As the children's skills develop, I progress to more taxing games involving the use of contents pages, indices, glossaries and encyclopaedias.

Having gone through a specimen lesson with the parents, I felt I could leave them to carry on in like manner without my assistance in the following weeks, matching the work more to their own child's particular interests and stage of development, which would be even better. We ended the morning session by reading together, child to parent, parent to child. For parents with two children the pattern, like mine, would be with a small group. One child would read silently while a second read with me. Or maybe they would listen to each other, or find a second copy of the same book and read in a pair, helping each other with strategies when unsure of a word. Then you could have a three-way discussion about the story at the end.

Thus we progressed until the end of term, doing it as a split class, half in the library and half in the classroom. I had planned to spend some time with each pair during the term, while also expecting to have to answer any sudden cries for help should they arise. It did not work out quite like that in reality. Although most parents felt confident enough to jump in, make mistakes, improve their technique as they went along (as I still do, as a teacher), I sensed that one or two were worried about being less than perfect, despite my initial handout and subsequent reassurances that nothing we were likely to do would be irrevocable. Not worrying is easier said than done, I know. So, I acted as role model and read with anxious parents, when the need arose.

At times, messages would come that Mum would be late as the baby had not woken up yet or had had to dash to the shops, or that dad had overslept. I stood in till the real parent arrived. Similarly, on occasions, parents had to leave early for an appointment, so again I took over as substitute parent. On even rarer occasions, a parent was unable to make it at all so I leapt into the breach for the whole session. At the end of the term, we had to take stock and decide what to do next. Give up or carry on?

Gathering momentum

Although no formal monitoring had taken place, it seemed obvious that children, parents and the school were enthusiastic enough for the project to continue for the next term. Parents who had been anxious about their child's progress were reassured by seeing for themselves that it was perfectly normal for children to develop in different ways at different times, to forge ahead, to plateau, to move slowly forward. Nobody can do 'their best' all day, every day.

Qualms about professional demarcation lines had not been an issue. We had not felt it necessary to split hairs about me doing the 'diagnostic reading' and the parents the 'practising reading'! As the class teacher I had responsibility for the organization of the whole class. No parent would ever have that. As parents, they had a unique contribution to make that no teacher could ever match. Also, for one morning a week at least, the children were hearing natural adult conversation about schoolwork instead of the somewhat artificial teacher-child version. It is not for nothing that recommendations have been made for always having two adults in classrooms.

Concern had been expressed about maths at one of the four curriculum evenings . . . some confusion about what a maths syllabus entailed these days and about how it was taught, some anxiety about progress rate and about children's lack of enthusiasm for the subject. As a staff we were keen to show that we were taking parents' comments seriously and were prepared, indeed eager, to put our house in order and try to improve our performance. Thus the head and I thought it would be appropriate to centre the next term's parents' mornings round computational maths.

I realized that we would have enough time to devote some to reading together as in the previous term, a little to handwriting and the rest to maths. Parents of the new intake children had heard about the project at the initial meeting at school and also, I suspect, from other parents involved, and were ready to make the weekly commitment. We needed only one introductory session while the head took my class as before.

We quickly recapped how to handle reading time. Then we moved on to how best to help with handwriting, where to start each letter, the actual letter formation, keeping the pencil in contact with the paper until the letter was complete, aiming for easy fluent action. We stressed the need to watch carefully as there is no guarantee that children will instinctively start in the right place or move in the right direction. Most of all we stressed that the most important thing was for the children to enjoy the experience.

Then we looked in detail at the new maths cards we had just bought, how they were grouped round particular concepts. We looked at maths apparatus giving examples of how children use them. We reminded parents that the school policy was for each group to have a maths teaching session each week then to practise that in subsequent days with the help of the cards, so that no one should be working from a position of failure or bewilderment. Finally, we went over the management details about how to find the cards you needed and what to do with them after you had finished your work.

We had a role-play session with a parent acting as a child reading the card to me, discussing how to tackle the problems posed, then recording the work, if necessary, and showing me the completed work. I stressed flexibility as there is no need to insist on recording if, for instance, a child was tiring, and it made more sense for the parent to take over. (On the other hand, if any writing or drawing were done, then it would be important to expect as high a standard as the child could manage.) I pointed out the rubber stamps, the cut-outs, the toys . . . all the things that might make life easier according to the needs and tastes of their particular child.

I decided to make Thursday my maths teaching point day so

that parents could see exactly what I do as a teacher, as well as what I expect the children to do. I altered my timetable accordingly. The art table was the only area big enough to seat a group of children, their parents, and me comfortably so that is where we gathered for the formal group maths teaching session – introducing subtraction, place value, counting in tens and the like, whatever stage the children happened to be at. Parents watched, helped, took a turn of their own as they saw fit. It was pleasing to note one girl telling her father off for holding the ten rods in his right hand and piling up units on the left! Needless to say, we could always be interrupted if any queries arose from the pairs working on their card assignments.

This meant that the art table was out of action for the morning, which was not ideal, and that the afternoon was spent finishing off bits and pieces on an *ad hoc* basis. It also made Thursday a fairly chaotic-looking day to an outsider, I imagine. I often wondered what students from the local college on one-day visits must have thought!

I found it an extremely interesting term. It was salutary to see parents looking puzzled or making the odd mistake, a reminder of how muddled explanations can become if we are not vigilant, of just how important the language of maths is and of how much we expect of children. It was wonderful to see parents' comments written in maths books, comments to me, at times, to explain or to query something; comments to the child beside mine, giving praise and encouragement. As I have said before, what a difference it makes to children when someone responds to their efforts, and maths work should be no exception to the rule.

Parents' comments to me afterwards were fascinating too. Some said they understood for the first time what maths was all about. The majority said again how good it was to be involved in their childen's normal working day. Others had enjoyed sharing in their child's excitement when they had grasped a new concept, or their pleasure at progressing to more complicated work.

There were moments of tension too, when parent and child were temperamentally divergent and an active parent wanted to urge a ruminant offspring to get the work finished. And there was one dissenting voice, a parent who felt she had no significant role to play other than a supervisory one and that her time could have been more profitably spent with her child working in another curriculum area. A perfectly valid point. Not everything works for every child-parent partnership. I was only sorry not to have picked it up sooner. Then, perhaps, we could have found a way round the problem together.

On the whole, feedback from the parents suggested that the advantages far outweighed the disadvantages. From the children, I got the impression that the important thing was that their parent or parent substitute was with them and the specific piece of work they were engaged in was of far less importance to them.

By the end of the term, we had been informed that we were to have a final teaching-practice student for the following term, one who had experienced some difficulties previously. The school, therefore, decided to cancel the parents' project for the coming term. It was not an easy decision – we were worried about losing momentum and about the new parents not getting into the habit of making a commitment right from the start. It was a fair one though. It would certainly have proved difficult for a student to cope with the extra organization, questioning looks, the toddlers, the unexpected incidents.

Back in the swim of things

It was good to learn that the gap had not adversely affected the parents when parents' mornings started again in the spring term. Parents were raring to get back into the classroom. Certainly the children were ready: they had never stopped asking when their parents were coming back to help again.

To follow sharing and choosing books, and maths, writing seemed the obvious next choice. More and more I had the feeling that writing, although overshadowed by reading for some years, was crucial to a child's success and enjoyment of school. I was very excited, then, about the term ahead. After the rather haphazard term on maths, I thought parents might appreciate a planned programme, so for their sake, I made out a list of activities for the entire term. This jarred somewhat with my beliefs about how best to encourage children to write. In my experience, people write best when they decide on the topic for themselves and are made to feel that their thoughts, feelings, anecdotes are of value to readers. Yet there I was ready to impose a pre-determined programme on the class!

I salved my conscience by reminding myself that it was for only one morning a week, and that there were plenty of other opportunities for the children to pursue their own writing themes. I did make a pact with the parents, though, to keep the programme a secret from the children so that they would not feel any sense of being coerced through a set pattern. And there was always the proviso that anyone adamantly opposed to any of the ideas could go their own way.

At the introductory meeting I distributed handouts suggesting various starting-points for writing and talked through the items listed. Then we discussed strategies for helping the children, depending on their degree of efficiency, with the content of their ideas and with the business of getting those ideas onto paper in a legible and comprehensible way. I stressed that of the two roles, that of creator is of paramount importance and must take priority over the role of secretary or scribe. Editing must be left till last, as with real publications when a publisher's copy editor will tidy up spelling and punctuation for authors.

We discussed the major temptation for an adult helper, that of wanting to impose one's own views on the writer. I, too, find that hardest of all and it has taken me a very long time to learn to stand back and give the children time to come to their own decisions. We just have to keep on reminding ourselves that it is the child's piece of writing, not ours . . . we can do our own alongside, if we like.

We needed to talk about the school's position on dialect too, in case parents leapt in and corrected features before a child was ready to take it on board. This is true of second-language learners as well. It needs an act of faith in children's ability to learn at their own pace. This is something they all do as long as they are not confused in the early days or given the impression by an adult that they are failing. Attitudes, as always, are vital and potentially the most difficult area to tackle. However, we were lucky in that all the parents seemed happy to comply with those views – in theory, at least!

Next we considered *Breakthrough to Literacy:*[1] how it combines all four language arts – listening, talking, reading, writing; how crucial the initial oral dialogue is for children to rehearse what they want to write and how exactly they want to express their thoughts and feelings in words; the routine of fetching words from the storage boxes; where to find card to write non-*Breakthrough* words; the importance of sensitively redrafting and finally editing the text in the stands with the child; deciding who would transcribe the finished product; encouraging attention to detail in accompanying drawings, if any; making sure words were put away in their folders afterwards.

Flexibility was stressed once again. There is no point in forcing exhausted young authors to write the whole story out themselves. If a child cannot face writing out vast quantities, there is nothing wrong with someone else acting as their secretary. As long as we hang on to the fact that the aim is for children to see themselves as writers and to enjoy composing and to want to keep on doing it, then we cannot go far wrong. Any suggestion that writing is a chore, a hassle, is to be avoided. Over the years children's stamina builds up in easy stages and they take on more and more of the secretary's tasks themselves, so there is no need to worry that children will *never* be able to write at length for themselves if we allow them to opt out of transcribing at the moment. Just the opposite in fact.

This was the third term of the project and I noticed how relaxed the parents who had been there from the start were, going straight into a routine and carrying the new parents along with them. It was extremely gratifying to see them begin to act independently rather than always looking to me for permission. They were quite at home not only fetching more card for *Breakthrough*, unearthing black felt tips for writing, but also in more important issues such as answering children's queries, discussing work with other people's children as well as their own, giving praise, reading completed stories.

For the first time there were some group activities, which was a big step forward. The children had shared story-writing before in pairs or in twos and threes round the computer-as-word-processor, but it was especially pleasing to see parents' and children's heads together working on a communal effort with sets of picture cards, or creating funny stories centred on a specific letter of the alphabet.

There were some unexpected bonuses. One parent had a newly acquired word processor and volunteered to bring it into school to print the class newspaper. It was a resounding success. The children gathered round to vote on size and type of print, layout and so forth. It was all carried out by the parents, printed and sold by them, while I carried on with the normal work of the classroom.

The children had found such pleasure in writing that they decided to found their own publishing firm. One boy designed the logo and printed it to put on all our publications and other children designed jacket covers. Parents undertook to assemble the books once we had the texts typed, to cover the backs, and to make a variety of bindings.

There was a boost for the hemiplegic girl in the class as the special typewriter she had to encourage her to use her left hand and to take the strain out of transcribing was much in demand for our publishing firm. That gave her enormous kudos as she had then to be in charge of the 'editor's office'.

With all these books pouring from the presses, I decided to take up an idea I had come across in *Practical Ways to Teach Writing*.[2] In the past we had featured 'author of the month' displays in the library but with 'real' authors of children's books. Now I chose one of the children to be author of the week. (I could engineer it so that over the two years they stayed in my class every one would have a turn!) The author composed a brief biography which was mounted on the board next to a photo and excerpts from their work. I bought a book for the chosen author from the school bookshop as a sort of Booker prize.

My worst fear at the very beginning of the project had been that the very young siblings accompanying parents would create problems by causing upheaval in the classroom, by weeping and wailing, and disturbing the workers or, at worst, by being involved in nasty accidents or getting lost. None of these things happened. They became so at home that they started a kind of playgroup of their own, which they organized themselves. Friendships flourished and they more or less ignored the rest of us. It quite staggered me. I am certain that it must have influenced their feelings towards going to school enormously. There were benefits for the older children, too. One of my lasting images is of six-year-old Diego's sudden shriek, 'Look, everyone! My baby's crawling!' All of us – parents, children, teacher – stopped what we were doing to share in the excitement at his brother's newly acquired skill and to applaud the baby!

At the end of term I sensed a great feeling of achievement from one and all. The parents and I, in a joint venture, led an assembly for the whole school sharing with them the work we had done. We got so enthusiastic that we overran the normal twenty minutes and went on for over an hour! Despite the timid voices of some of the five-year olds, they held the attention of even the notorious section of the fourth year juniors, which speaks for itself.

Several of the parents were hooked on the whole question of literacy by now and on children's literature. They joined staff and children for a trip to the public library to hear the New Zealand author, Lynley Dodd, talk about her work. We all finished up in a publication about librarians! Later, when Frank Smith talked about the reading process at the university, nine of our parents turned up to buy tickets. Many a school would have had difficulty getting their staff to spend two hours towards the end of the summer term listening to an educational discourse, never mind the parents. With that level of commitment, it looked as if parents' mornings were well and truly here to stay.

Feeling at home

Better late than never, and spurred on by my recent observations of parents' considerable abilities, I realized that I had been making all the decisions, either on my own or in consultation with the head. It was high time parents got a look in at the planning stage. What transpired was not an ideal forum for discussion. It was a fairly quick consultation over coffee on the last parents' morning of term, with a dozen or so parents who had been able to stay on after the session had ended. One parent suggested topic maths, and the rest agreed so that was that. The reading would run on as before.

The maths support teacher, assigned to the school, was continuing to work in tandem with class teachers, a term at a time. It seemed sensible for me to take my turn now so that the support teacher could work on practical maths with the parents. Guided by her, we decided to devote the term to measuring. She would work with the younger children in the class, concentrating on weighing in the first half term and length in the second half. I was to tackle time with the older children.

The pattern varied from week to week. Sometimes my groups gathered *en masse* to brainstorm sayings connected with time.

144

Sometimes I launched the morning's work orally, then parents and children went off in pairs, for instance, doing a personal life line. Sometimes – and this was an innovation for the parents – I gave out lesson guidelines to them so that they could lead the discussion and organize activities such as making a pie chart about how you spend your day. Sometimes I gave written instructions to the children, for instance for tasks to be carried out in the playground set against the stop watch, on the understanding that their parents would co-operate. I had learned to trust parents by then: their handling of their own children in school as opposed to at home, their handling of unexpected situations and of educational issues.

Of course, they made mistakes, but so did I. For instance, I do wish it had occurred to me to invite the maths support teacher and the parents for a get-together before the start of term. It would have been helpful, especially as she had never worked with parents in this way before. However, I was delighted to hear from her later that she had introduced the idea of parents' mornings to her school. It was a relief to learn that my throwing her in at the deep end like that had not put her off the idea for life!

Again there were unforeseen benefits. Parents had always looked at display boards first thing in the morning but now they started to add things where appropriate, helping children to fill in sections on moving house, which was the term's theme. They took part wholeheartedly in the questionnaire the children devised about reasons for moving and had a hand in the final block graph.

One completely unexpected spin-off was how the parents helped me to make up my mind about the 'real books' debate. We had changed to individualized reading when I had first arrived at the school in 1980 and the books had been colour coded since then. I had begun to feel uneasy that this system had not completely eliminated competition between children. Most of all, I was becoming increasingly uneasy about the quality of some of the texts, especially those for inexperienced readers. For some time I had been toying with the idea of introducing the apprenticeship model for learning to read advocated by teachers such as Liz Waterland.[3] I was hesitating because I was having difficulty working out how to organize the change-over.

Over coffee each week the parents and I aired our views about education in general. Disaffection with colour coding, it turned

out, was worrying parents, too. After chewing over various alter-
natives, we decided to have a trial run of 'anything goes'. The
school bought a lot of new paperbacks and I left boxes of all
sorts of books – spotted, unspotted, and mixtures – around the
classroom. By the end of the term it seemed to me that all the
children had thoroughly enjoyed making their own decisions about
what to read. I could see no adverse effects in any of the children.

Two incidents clinched it for me. One child who could read
quite well was simply not hooked on books: he could take them
or leave them. *Angry Arthur* (Oram 1984) proved to be the breakthrough for him. After that he was never without a book in his
hand. Another child had been worrying me considerably for some
time. Over the two terms he had been in school, his involvement
with books had developed very little, which was rare. He was the
only child who had ever said to me, 'I can't read', and this had
shaken me badly. One day he pounced on *Better Move on Frog*
(Maris 1984). For the first time, his eyes lit up as he read it with
confidence, read and reread it, chortled over it with a friend and
read it again. Eventually, and reluctantly, he was persuaded to
put it in 'the going home box' with all the other books that children
would take home that night to share with their families. 'Real'
books had proved their worth.

What was it exactly in those discussions with parents that pushed
me over that stumbling block? Was it hearing that the parents
were experiencing a similar disillusionment to mine? Was it just
being able to use a larger number of people than usual as a
sounding board? Was it that I felt their support and their trust in
me personally that gave me the confidence to have a crack at it?
I am not sure. But what I was sure about was that we had a
real partnership now, in the best sense, with everybody reaping
benefits.

What about us?

It had not gone unnoticed by the parents of the other two Infant
classes that the parents' project had grown into an established
tradition and that parents, children and teacher were finding it
great fun. As you can imagine, after a couple of terms, the other
Infant children and their parents were asking when it would be
their turn. We had always intended to extend the project, if

successful, and the other two teachers were keen to be involved. Thus with everyone's agreement parents' mornings were extended throughout the Infant department. The others followed the same pattern as my class for the first term until they found their feet and went on to develop their own ways of doing things. Inevitably, systems of organization differ from one teacher to another. So does interaction with parents, as individual personalities lead to different emphases, different styles.

Now that all three Infant classes had parents in for a morning each, the staff-room was overcrowded three mornings out of five. Given that each teacher does playground duty once a week, some teachers could find a calm, peaceful staff-room to relax in only for one morning. It was decided to abandon the practice of parents taking coffee in the staff-room and transfer to the classroom instead. The parents accepted it as perfectly reasonable. Many of them help out singly at other times with a variety of activities and join the teachers in the staff-room then, so they know that it is not forbidden territory

These days there is more co-operation and exchange of ideas about parents' mornings. Some of the past mistakes have been rectified – for instance, ensuring that interpreters are present at the initial meeting. Also, termly evaluation as to which activities are preferred, whether to alter the organization, the type of work, whether to work with another child instead of your own . . . all this is discussed openly and taken into consideration before planning the next term's work. There have been further attempts to include parents in the decision-making by offering a choice of four or five activities for the individual parent to opt for, according to his or her own preference, but we still offer precise tasks for those parents who feel happier working that way.

We feel we were right to start small and grow, rather than rush into a grand scheme involving several classes straightaway. There might also be a case for caution in the case of teachers either new to the school or new to the profession. It has to be said that, if parents' mornings are to be successful, they involve teachers in a substantial amount of planning and organization and it might be unrealistic to expect teachers already coping with settling into a new job and building up relationships with children, staff, and parents, to take on any extra commitments.

Where next?

Parent's mornings have played a very important part in the development of parental involvement in Redlands and new questions surface all the time. For instance, should parents be free to come into school to work with their children on any morning that suits them? (This suggestion is not as impractical as it might first seem. It is most unlikely that teachers would be coping with a roomful of parents every day!) In practice, it had not proved at all difficult to make arrangements for individual needs. One parent came in daily for half a term to work with her son on his maths. She needed to make sure that he would be able to cope with the tests which he would have to face when he went back to South Africa at the end of the year. Another parent has triplets and has chosen to place them in three separate classes. Obviously she will have to work with each of her children at times which are convenient for her.

I also wonder if we have reached the stage when we can leave decisions to each individual parent and child team to formulate their own programme of work for the term instead of imposing the same theme or set of activities on everyone? There would still be room for those who prefer to work together as a group on the same topic. Finally, we are aware of how important it is to keep our eyes and ears open for exciting initiatives elsewhere. The National Writing Project and the Oracy Project, for instance, have already influenced our discussions on future plans.

In short . . .

There has been nothing in our experience to suggest that some areas of the curriculum are better suited to parental involvement than others. Parents' mornings have covered most areas – maths, language, topic, science, art – and parents have been able to make a valuable contribution to the whole range. Needless to say, different parent-child partnerships prefer different kinds of activities, but flexibility on the part of the teacher can accommodate their preferences without difficulty. As the project is still in an early stage of development, there will be plenty of opportunity for negotiating with parents the arrangements that suit them best.

Naturally, parents' mornings have not been without their share of frustrations. Sometimes, parents have to come to terms with the worries that comparing their own children's performance with others can bring; sometimes they have difficulty disguising their natural, human annoyance when children do not perform as they expect. On balance, though, the benefits of parents' mornings far outweigh the frustrations. The opportunity to work with children in the classroom in this way clearly gives the parents an accurate picture not only of *what* but *how* their children are learning at school. It thus demystifies the process, removing a great deal of misunderstanding and confusion.

It also has the effect of cementing relationships – with children who are obviously thrilled to have their parents in the classroom; with their children's friends; relationships with each other; and, not least, with the teacher who becomes a friend known by her first name, who can be chatted to, questioned, appealed to, winked at, cried all over, and hugged.

Parents' voices

Getting started . . .

- You feel a bit shy and unsure at first, but you soon get the hang of it.
- I needed more guidance in the early days on how to behave in the classroom. Should I let my own child go his own way or try to guide him? Was I supposed to keep an eye on just my own child or should I keep others in line, too?
- Maybe we could observe how the teacher does things the first week before having to join in actively.
- I needed to feel very clear about what we were doing and why, in order to feel less uncertain. But I found that confidence in dealing with children did grow over the weeks.

Learning about learning

- It's great to keep in touch with the exact stage your child is at. It makes it easier to encourage in specific directions.
- It's important to see the new methods of teaching reading and doing maths actually at work in the classroom, because it was all different from when I was at school.

- I thoroughly enjoyed the group work and the feeling that we were enabling things to happen that couldn't happen so easily without us. We weren't just 'minding' the children!
- It's wonderful for people like me who know nothing about education. I'm really keen for my children to do well. It's important for parents to see what's going on, though. I learnt such a lot from parents' mornings. When you first go in you see your child can't read or write and you think, 'Oh, Lord! However are they going to learn all that?' You want it all to happen quickly and you get anxious. Then you realize that they do learn, but it's a gradual process. Parents can create problems if we're not careful because we're so tense and we expect too much too soon. I learnt to be more tolerant, more patient – even at home, too. I learnt a lot. Now with my second child I've got a completely different approach. I know he'll be alright. I can strike a happy medium and not be too pushy.
- It's a good idea to find out what's going on in school.
- I enjoy the weekly sessions. I know exactly what my son is doing. It's quite different somehow from popping in and out at the start of the day and at home time. You're involved with all the details.
- It was a lot of fun. The excitement of the children when something was produced co-operatively was infectious.
- Benefits: an opportunity to see at first hand how your child is doing.
- It was interesting to see how the age-range is taught.
- When parents were in the classroom we felt more positive and enthusiastic when we were part of a team working alongside/with the teacher – not separate. We were not there simply to observe our own child's behaviour to see how they approached work but were playing an active and useful role in the classroom and, in particular, in our child's education.
- Parents' mornings are a very rewarding way of seeing your children's education from the other side.

Relationships
- You get a really good relationship with the teacher. It makes it easy to ask her things, question things. It doesn't seem like complaining any more.

- Many parents felt the experience helped them to understand the teachers' job, to appreciate his/her special skills. (It also allowed parents to identify any shortcomings with justification rather than supposition.)
- I find that parents seem to find the teachers much more approachable because of these mornings. (Perhaps the reverse is true as well?) I also feel that the morale of the school as a whole is raised immeasurably as a result. The parents and grandparents in my daughter's class are from astonishingly varied backgrounds but they are very friendly towards each other in that shared environment. I feel it helps to develop a genuine community spirit in the neighbourhood.
- I realized it was very, very important for my daughter to have me there. There was no way I could miss a morning. So, I suppose, in a way I did feel under pressure to go. I'd have felt guilty otherwise. But I always enjoy it.
- The child very much enjoys you being there. If, through circumstances, a parent is unable to be there on a regular basis, the child doesn't seem to suffer and enjoys reading etc. to a friend's parent and maybe looks forward more to the times you *can* come in.
- It was very important to my son that I was there – I always had to have a sound reason for absence.
- Working parents may feel concerned that parents' mornings will mean their child will be the odd one out and in some way disadvantaged. There seems to be considerable reluctance on the part of parents to ask friends (other than those with children in the same class) or neighbours to stand in.
- I've enjoyed getting access to the whole range of work and I think I've learned something about my son's personality, aptitudes, abilities and problems in the process.
- It's nice to get to know the other children who are part of my daughter's life.
- It was a great pleasure working with my son in the classroom, seeing how he enjoyed his work, helping him with it, seeing how he related to other children and to his teacher.
- It was lovely to have such a cheerful atmosphere. That's good for the children and for us parents as well.
- My husband enjoyed parents' mornings a lot. He's lucky, he's

got a job where he can come along. Lots of fathers can't and that's a shame.

- I find the experience of parents' mornings worthwhile and it is refreshing to belong to a school that welcomes parental contributions.

Younger children . . .

- At times there were disadvantages in having younger children hanging round your knees when you were trying to read a story. That was nothing in comparison with what you gained.
- The atmosphere in the classroom is lovely, especially with babies and toddlers around. Any children who don't have younger brothers and sisters really benefit from the contact and only children get to share other children's little ones.
- My two pre-school children enjoyed it as much as me. 'We're going to Andrew's class today, Mummy, aren't we? We're going to see his teacher.' I'm sure this is why my next son settled so well into nursery – he knew his way round the school from parents' mornings. He was used to being there and wandering round. He knew all the teachers from being in the staff room.
- Smaller children are welcomed on these mornings. However, caring for some children, particularly those between 18 months and 4 years can be a real strain in that situation. I don't like taking my boisterous two-year-old along. (The last time he nearly ran the headteacher over – she laughed, fortunately!) Therefore I do a child swap with another mother in a similar situation. This is very time-consuming. A crèche would be very welcome.

Frustrations

- You can't help yourself comparing your child's progress with other children. You have to keep reminding yourself that what the teacher says is true – they all learn in different ways at different rates, but they get there in the end.
- It was a shock at first. I used to compare my child's progress though I knew I shouldn't. I wish I knew then what I know

now. If I could go back and start again, I'd approach it quite differently. I have learnt so much.

- At times there was some friction between my expectations and my child's responses

- I think many parents feel inside that they are back in the classroom as they were as a child – i.e. they want to please the teacher with the work produced. There is also the anxiety/ pride in the child himself – that you want him to please the teacher – so there is the temptation to mould his work to what you believe is a 'higher standard', but which, of course, is no longer 'him' so much as 'you'. I had to stop myself doing this!

- Sometimes I felt that I was holding my kids back, that some days they produced less work than they normally would. I'm sure that there were many other unseen benefits but I found it hard to keep that in perspective sometimes.

- Sometimes I felt like a taskmaster pleading and cajoling to make sure that my kids got through a respectable amount of work.

- I was keen to have half an hour one-to-one with my son and sometimes that wasn't possible if the work was group-based. We both found that frustrating.

- Helping with the reading and language was much easier for me. In my opinion the maths was a disaster. I would prefer to read and then do some project work.

- Working one-to-one, sometimes I felt pressure on me and on the child – like at home! It was easier with group activities and I think my son enjoyed that more, too. But I learned how to cope with the frustrations and I think he learned what he would and would not get away with.

- Working with your own child and his/her friend can cause competition and squabbling between them. My daughter's teacher has solved this by announcing the name of individual children who will be working with her or her helper and saying the rest will work with their parents.

- I only went once. My son hated it. He was dreadful . . . uncooperative, generally frustrating. I didn't enjoy the experience at all. My husband's been every other time. They do some wonderful things together. It's nice for other children to see an ordinary man in the infants as well.

Moving on . . .

- I would like to end the session with the parents reading stories to the class so that we all finished on a high note.
- Personally, I might prefer to give someone else's child individual attention – although my son definitely wouldn't prefer that!
- Would it be possible to change the day from time to time, termly maybe, so that parents unable to come regularly on one particular day get a chance to share in the sessions?
- It's more satisfying for parents to feel really involved, rather than simply supervising day-to-day activities. I think we should avoid using the session for normal work. It's better when we switch tasks and have a variety from week to week.
- I would like time at the beginning of each session to go through the week's work in my son's tray to see what he's been doing. I know we can do that at any time but usually my younger children are hanging round me first thing in the morning and it's not a good moment.
- I wish we could be staggered through the week and perhaps choose our own time to come and work with our child, and generally assist in the classroom as well.

Children's voices

Who comes . . .

- My mum couldn't come very often but I still looked forward to it.
- I felt sad sometimes when my mum couldn't come but it was OK with somebody else's mum.
- Thursday was always the very best day because my mum came.
- I wished my mum could come to parents' mornings. Sometimes my big sister came.
- My mum works full-time so another mum helps me.
- My daddy came to parents' mornings once when he didn't have to go to work so early. Or maybe he was on holiday. Anyway, he came.
- Beji (grandma) only comes when she wants to. Now she's

gone to Birmingham, but she's going to come back. She likes
to see my work and how I'm getting on. I tell her in Panjabi
what it is. I like it when my dad comes, too, but he hasn't
got much time.

What I liked best . . .

- My mum helped me so well when I did my stories. There was
  about ten chapters once – it was excellent, that story.
- On parents' mornings you could do anything you liked –
  maths, reading, story, handwriting, choosing, art – anything.
  Mum liked reading best but I thought it was all good.
  Sometimes she got a bit cross with me.
- I like doing art best with my mum. The bit I didn't like was
  when they went home.
- I like doing maths together best. I really like maths.
- I know the really good bit. It was doing floating and sinking
  with all the mums there.
- Why do I like parents' mornings? Mmmm . . . it's just nice
  to see my mum in school, you know. I like her to be here
  because she helps me and I think it's really good. She gets to
  know all the children because she didn't know them before.

Younger children

- My little brothers just went and played in the home corner
  on parents' morning all the time. You didn't have to tell
  them off or anything. My mum said it was marvellous.
- My baby enjoyed it. He'd never been to school before. It
  interrupted my work a little bit, but it didn't matter.
- I went to parents' mornings with my daddy even before I
  started school because I was in the nursery in the afternoons.
  I got to know all my sister's friends and they read to me.
  When I got bored I played in the home corner.

Moving on . . .

- I'd like them to stay longer – till lunch time. Well, you could
  even have Parents' *Day*!
- We don't have parents' mornings in the juniors. It would be

nice. I'd still like it. When I've got a hard piece of work to do, I need my mum. Sometimes I couldn't do it by myself, I just couldn't get it right.

- Parents ought to come in on other times. We were playing on the computer and some of the things were really hard. We needed them then.
- We don't have parents' mornings anymore but my mum still comes in. My favourite is when she does consultations and publishing my stories.
- When we do 'writers' workshop' with Alex's mum or Brendan's mum, they can spend more time with you than a teacher.

Chapter 11

Parents as partners,

We have reached an interesting stage at Redlands. We are confident of the value of involving parents fully in the life of the school and have the full backing of parents, teachers and governors for this policy. We have learned to trust parents, both for their good sense and their commitment to their children's well-being in school. There can be no doubt that we have made our fair share of mistakes. We will no doubt continue to make them. It seems to us, though, that mistakes can be forgiven in an atmosphere in which parents and teachers respect one another, where there is a genuine will to try and do better and to accommodate everybody's needs and interests.

One of the main areas where we have sometimes made quite wrong assumptions is in believing that the teachers are always the ones who are best qualified to make all the decisions about what should be done, how and when. Yet, we have found repeatedly that when we take the time to talk to parents about a particular question, the parents' perspective has quite often helped us see things much more clearly and has led in the long term to a much more satisfactory solution. Even if there has been no clear consensus of opinion between parents and teachers, we have at least been able to respect each other's positions and to deal more honestly with each other.

The feeling of trust which can be built up by recognizing that parents are equal partners in their children's education opens the way for a whole range of questions, questions which would have been unimaginable even a short time ago. It also helps us think more critically of what we have achieved in Redlands and the areas where we really need to do more serious thinking.

Going to waste

If we are really serious about drawing on parents' skills and expertise, what precisely are we doing about it? Until now, we have asked for help from parents when we know they have a particular skill that fits in with the work we are doing. Almost certainly, a great deal of expertise is still being lost. One possible way of dealing with this would be to invite parents to take part in the planning activities. Perhaps towards the second half of each term, parents and teacher could decide on which aspects of the school theme they would like to concentrate on in the following term and work out the programme accordingly. Then parents, teachers, and class could follow this up with a brainstorming session. In this way, parents might be more likely to offer their talents and ensure that they are incorporated in school projects.

Mary Martyn-Johns introduced a planned programme of school-based in-service for staff every Wednesday from 3.15 to 5.00 p.m. As well as advancing curriculum development and personal staff development, it has been instrumental in cementing teacher relationships. At the beginning of the school year in 1987, parent governors and representatives from the PTA were invited for the first time to join with staff as they considered whether to abandon colour coding throughout the school and shift totally to 'real books'. This proved to be a great success, with parents fully relaxed and entering into the debate wholeheartedly, and there is obviously much scope for further development in this direction. For instance, Redlands has been involved in an initiative to link five inner-town schools for mutual evaluation. It would be interesting to add another dimension and link the parents of the schools so that ideas on parental involvement could be shared to everyone's advantage.

What's missing?

An objective look at who actually comes to help in school hours reveals that it is mostly women – mothers, grandmothers, big sisters. Admittedly, there is no reluctance on the part of fathers to come in whenever they are free, and grandfathers appear on the odd occasion, too. The situation is not helped by the fact that there are few male teachers in infant classrooms. This raises all kinds of worries about the range of role models we are offering the children, although we are constantly looking for ways to challenge stereotypes. One small illustration: the teaching staff have traditionally served the Christmas dinner to the children. For two years we were an all-female staff and we were not happy with the kitchen sink and apron image. So the caretaker, plus those of our husbands near enough to get to us in their lunch break, did the serving. We clearly need to think carefully about the hidden messages in what we do and say.

And what about ethnic-minority parents? The parents who talked to us when we were researching this book expressed satisfaction that the school and the curriculum are responding to their needs and interests. But to what extent do ethnic-minority parents feel as involved in the life of the school as other parents? This seems to vary from family to family. While we have made a great deal of progress in many areas, we are aware that this issue is seen very much from the perspective of a predominantly white staff and we must ensure a platform for all parents to speak for themselves about their needs and preferences.

Getting an accurate picture

We definitely need more careful monitoring and evaluation of what we are achieving and hope to achieve in the short and long term. It is very easy as a teacher to think that everything is going well, but it is only when all parties – parents, children and teachers – are given the opportunity to share their views openly and honestly that we can build up an accurate picture of the effectiveness or otherwise of what we are doing.

One of the exciting aspects of writing this book has been talking to parents and children at length about what we have been doing. It has, of course, confirmed our own view of the value of involving parents in the life of the school, but it has also highlighted areas of concern that still need to be resolved. One such area is the discrepancy in the school's approach to literacy and numeracy: children are encouraged to take home books each night to share with their families, while there is an embargo on taking home maths cards and no machinery for borrowing maths games. The frequency with which children referred to maths in worried tones has pinpointed this as an issue that parents and teachers need to devote considerable time to in the near future. We are hoping, for instance, to start a programme along the lines of IMPACT[1] where children and parents can take part in mathematical games and activities together at home.

Getting started

So what have we learned about working with parents at Redlands? Where some teachers are committed to the idea of partnership with parents but there is no well-established tradition in the school, how can they proceed? (The ideal situation of a school, which has a well thought out policy on parents and the whole staff are in agreement, is something of a rarity.) It seems to us, though, that it is possible to make a start in this direction without total commitment of this kind, as long as staff relationships are good and people are working well as a team. Obviously, the head-teacher must be in favour of involving parents and, preferably, other senior teachers, too. All the same, it is not necessary for every class to be working in the same way at the same time. It may even be advisable, at times, to start small and then expand.

In this way it is possible for colleagues to gain in confidence. It is far more persuasive to see something working well in the next classroom – to realize that the chaos and confusion which you thought a particular project might involve does not actually materialize – than to be told that this is the school's policy and that this is therefore what you, too, will do. This slow but sure approach also allows you to learn from other people's mistakes when things go wrong! It is very important for people to be allowed to feel their way into a situation and gradually mould it into something which feels comfortable for them.

This raises another question. If some teachers in a school are involving parents more actively than others what is likely to be the end result? The most likely scenario, for purely historical reasons, is that infants teachers are working more closely with parents than their colleagues in the junior department. This was certainly the case in Redlands and we spent a great deal of time wondering what impact the initiatives in the infant department would have on the rest of the school.

When parents' mornings had become well-established and the first group of children were moving on to the junior department where far fewer parents were spending time, it proved to be no problem. Parents were so used to coming into school by that point that they felt no inhibitions about offering their services to the First Year junior teacher. Their involvement has taken a different tack. They come in ones and twos or small groups to help with 'writers' workshop' activities – consulting, redrafting, editing, publishing – as well as reading with children, helping with maths and a wide range of other activities, and they are now set to carry on working in this way as their children move on through the Junior department.

The next wave of parents involved in parents' mornings has shown a similar commitment. To cope with rising numbers, a Top infant class had to be created in 1987. As all downstairs rooms were already occupied, it had to be housed upstairs, the traditional home of the juniors. Mary Martyn-Johns had therefore assumed that parents' mornings, as such, would discontinue. During the first few weeks of the school year, however, she picked up feelings of disappointment from children and parents. She promptly sent out letters asking for clarification of their feelings on the subject. All but three parents were in favour of keeping up the commitment to parents' mornings, so they were quickly reinstated.

All parents receive a letter at the beginning of the year outlining areas where they may be prepared to offer regular help and inviting alternative suggestions. The majority of parents who reply have children in the infants. After all, many mothers of slightly older children take on full- or part-time work which makes a regular commitment impossible. None the less, we have a growing number of parents involved in activities with the juniors. We had thought to begin with that the older children might be embarrassed at their parents continuing to come into their classroom. It would seem that this is only a problem for children who are not used to working with parents. Children of all ages in Redlands have made it very clear that they enjoy having their parents in school.

Real partnership?

While we are mindful of the many shortcomings in what has been happening in Redlands, we are also very confident that the way in which partnership with parents at the school has been developing is very good for all concerned – parents, teachers and, above all, children. Schools like ours have now accumulated a great deal of experience about what is involved in working with parents, making it possible to speculate on what works well and why.

When a school opens its doors, it lays the foundations for a strong sense of the school as a community. Parents interact with other parents, their own children, their children's friends, their children's teachers. People see each other in a variety of roles, both inside and outside school hours. The feeling of belonging to a team which grows from this kind of contact breaks down the 'them and us' mentality and promotes an openness and trust which would not otherwise be possible.

The experience of meeting socially and working together has a number of important by-products: shared pleasure at working with your own and other people's children; shared excitement at children's progress and achievements; shared understanding of common aims and objectives; freedom to question and to express doubts when things do not go as hoped. The involvement which was made possible by good communication feeds, in turn, into even more effective communication.

The kind of development which we have been documenting for Redlands is, of course, by no means unique. Similar initiatives are to be found in many schools throughout the length and breadth of Britain. The fact remains, however, that some schools and teachers are considerably further forward in their thinking on parental involvement than others. Why does this happen?

For parental involvement to be a success, there needs to be a willingness to reconsider the traditional role of the teacher. As a result of their training and past expectations of society, some teachers may still believe that their task is to transmit knowledge to the children in their care. Teachers who consider themselves as the fount of all knowledge are more likely to feel anxious about involving parents in their children's schooling. Teachers have to be prepared to face their own prejudices, accept criticism and rethink the situation. For as we find out more about the learning process, we realize that teachers in school – and parents and others in the world outside – simply provide the right environment to interest and motivate children and facilitate their learning. In other words, we must place greater trust in the children's role as constant active learners.

The same is true of attitudes towards parents. Involving parents requires an act of faith to get started and a firm will to succeed. For a considerable time parents have been blamed for the poor achievement of their children in school and teachers have colluded with the widespread belief that many parents are unwilling or unable to help their children's learning. The evidence from Redlands and many other schools is overwhelming: give parents the opportunity and the encouragement and they will respond enthusiastically.

The fact of the matter is that parents offer a considerable pool of expertise across the curriculum which it would be foolhardy to overlook. They can also offer a perspective on the child which is beyond the reach of teachers and which teachers ignore at their own peril. The best decisions about a child are arrived at not by the teacher alone, but by the teacher in consultation with parents.

Likewise, decisions about the school: policy, organization, the curriculum, parental involvement – all these areas affect parents either directly or indirectly. Parents can provide a very valuable sounding board for new ideas; they can help identify problems and suggest alternative solutions. By offering parents a share in the decision-making process, a great deal of misunderstanding and anxiety is avoided, and the end result will be far more satisfactory for all concerned. In our experience, fears about parents taking over are completely misplaced. No matter how many parents help in no matter how many different ways, the ultimate responsibility for the classroom and all the children in it lies with the teacher, just as the ultimate responsibility for the school rests with the headteacher.

What we are talking about, then, is partnership with parents. All manner of partnerships spring to mind – business partners, marriage partners, sleeping partners, sparring partners . . . part-ners in crime! The balance of give and take fluctuates in all partnerships worthy of the name and home-school partnerships will be no exception. In all probability the teacher will take the lead most of the time, but not at the expense of parents' opinions or their expert knowledge of their own children.

In short . . .

There is no magic formula for success. We have tried to present a full and accurate picture of things which in the opinion of both parents and teachers have worked well for Redlands. We have also tried to look critically at the mistakes we have made and to identify areas where we need to think more carefully. All schools are different and should hang on to whatever works for them. School should be about feeling happy and developing a genuine interest in learning. Anything that pulls parents, teachers and children together in a bid to ensure that no child slips through the educational net cannot be bad.

Notes

Chapter 2 – Parents: help or hindrance?

1. Plowden, B. (1967) *Children and their Primary Schools*, London: HMSO.
2. See, for example, J. Hale (1972) 'Parent-teacher co-operation: an official view', in T.M. Cluderay (ed.) *Home and School Relationships*, special issue of *Aspects of Education* 15: 70–5.
3. Halsey. A.H. (ed.) (1972) *Educational Priority Volume 1: EPA Problems and Policies*, London: HMSO.
4. Bruner, J. (1974) *Beyond the Information Given*, London: Allen & Unwin.
5. Radin, N. (1972) 'Three degrees of maternal involvement in a pre-school program: impact on mothers and children', *Child Development* 43:1355–64.
6. Bernstein, B. (1973) *Class, Codes and Control*, Vol. 1, London: Routledge & Kegan Paul.
7. Bullock, Sir A. (1976) *A Language of Life*, London: HMSO.
8. Herbstein, D. (1980) 'I'm in need of smalltalk', *Sunday Times*, 27 January: 12.
9. Tough, J. (1985) *Talk Two*, London: Onyx Press.
10. Jackson, L. (1974) 'The myth of the elaborated and restricted code', *Higher Education Review* 6(2): 47, 49, 65.
11. Labov, W. (1973) 'The logic of non-standard English', in N. Keddie (ed.) *Tinker, Tailor . . . The Myth of Cultural Deprivation*, Harmondsworth: Penguin, pp. 21–66.
12. See, for instance, Wells, G. (1985) *Language Development in the Pre-School Years*, Cambridge: Cambridge University Press; (1987) *The Meaning Makers: Children Learning Language and Using Language to Learn*, London: Hodder & Stoughton.
13. Tizard, B. and Hughes, M. (1984) *Young Children Learning*, London: Fontana.
14. For an overview of this area, see V. Edwards (1983) *Language in Multicultural Classrooms*, London: Batsford.
15. L. Mercer (1981) 'Ethnicity and the supplementary school', in N. Mercer (ed.) *Language in School and Community*, London: Edward Arnold, pp. 147–60.
16. Quoted in Townsend, H.E.R. (1971) *Immigrants in England: the LEA Response*, Slough: National Foundation for Educational Research, p.60.
17. See, for instance, Centre for Contemporary Cultural Studies (1982) *The Empire Strikes Back: Race and Racism in 70s Britain*, London: Hutchinson;

Tomlinson, S. (1984) *Home and School in Multicultural Britain*, London; Batsford.

18. Stacey, M. (1985) 'Parent/teacher partnership: from rhetoric to reality', unpublished MPhil. thesis, Cranfield Institute of Technology.

19. For fuller discussion, see 'The evidence of case studies of parents' involvement in schools' by J. Hewison in C. Cullingford (ed.) (1985) *Parents, Teachers and Schools*, London: Robert Royce, pp. 41–60.

20. See, for example, C Athey (1981) 'Parental involvement in nursery education', *Early Child Development and Care*, 7 (4): 353–67; M. Prosser (1981) 'The myth of parental apathy', *Times Educational Supplement*, 16 October: 22–3; Rathbone, M. and Graham, N.C. (1981) 'Parent participation in the primary school', *Educational Studies* 7 (2): 145–50; Smith, T. (1980) *Parents and the Pre-School*, London: Grant McIntyre.

21. See, for example, Stone, M. (1980) *The Education of the Black Child in Britain*, London: Fontana; and Tomlinson, S. (1984) *Home and School in Multicultural Britain*, London: Batsford.

22. Bullock, Sir A. (1976) *A Language for Life*, London: HMSO; Taylor, T. (1977) *A New Partnership for our Schools*, London: HMSO; Warnock, M. (1978) *Special Educational Needs: Report of the Committee of Inquiry into the Education of Handicapped Children and Young Persons*, London: HMSO; Hargreaves, D. (1984) *Improving Secondary Schools: Report of the Committee on the Curriculum and Organisation of Secondary Schools*, London: ILEA; Swann, Lord (1985) *Education for All*, London: HMSO; Education, Science and Arts Committee (1986) *Achievement in Primary Schools*, Vol. 1, London: HMSO; ILEA (1985) *Improving Primary Schools: Report of the Committee on Primary Education*, London: ILEA.

Chapter 3 – Parents after Plowden

1. Cyster, R., Clift, P.S. and Battle S. (1979) *Parental Involvement in Primary Schools*, Slough: National Foundation for Educational Research.

2. For a discussion of the early history of PTAs see, for example, Goodacre, E. (1970) *Home and School*, Slough: National Foundation for Educational Research.

3. 1984 report by HM Inspectors on *The Effects of Local Authority Expenditure Policies on Education Provision in England in 1983*; and 1984 report by HM Inspectorate for Wales on *The Effects on the Education Service in Wales of Recent Local Authority Expenditure Policies* (covering the school year 1983–4).

4. National Confederation of Parent Teacher Associations (NCPTA) (1985) *The State of Schools in England and Wales. Crumbling schools: Fact or Fiction?; Parental Funding – How Much and What For?* Gravesend: NCPTA.

5. Scottish Parent Teacher Council (SPTC) (1983) *Ideas for an Active PTA*, Edinburgh: SPTC.

6. 'Parents see small classes as top need', *Times Educational Supplement* 21.11.1986: 10.

7. 'Bench-mark tests backlash threatened', *Times Educational Supplement*, 2.10.87: 1.

8. Milne, S. (1987) 'Inners and outers', *The Guardian*, 22 September: 13; 'Reveal those parents pushing for change, NAPE challenges', *Times Educational Supplement*, 9 October 1987: 8.

9. Blunkett, D. (1987) 'Facing up to the new realities', *Times Educational Supplement*, 25 October: 4.
10. Bastiani, J. (ed.) (1978) *Written Communication Between School and Home*, Nottingham: Nottingham University School of Education.
11. Originally reported by E. Goodacre in *Home and School* (NFER, 1970).
12. MacLeod, F. (1985) *Parents in Partnership* – Involving Muslim Parents in their Children's Education, Community Education Development Centre, Coventry; also *Parents are Welcome*, a video in English and Urdu, available from the Community Education Officer, LINCS, Lyford Road, Reading.
13. Taylor, T (1977) *A New Partnership for our Schools*, London: HMSO.
14. See, for example, Cullingford, C. (1985) 'Teachers, parents and the control of schools', in C. Cullingford (ed.) *Parents, Teachers and Schools*, London: Robert Royce, pp. 1–15; O'Connor, M. (1987) 'Parent Power', The Guardian, 31 March: 13; and Barker, R. (1987) 'Hidden factors governing the voice of parents', *The Guardian* 24 February: 13.
15. Sutcliffe, J. (1987) 'The sleeping giant begins to stir', *Times Educational Supplement*, 20 March: 7; Sutcliffe. J. (1987) 'Tightrope artists who have kept their balance', *Times Educational Supplement*, 17 April: 3.
16. David, H. (1986) 'Parent governors – elected or selected?' *Times Educational Supplement*, 3 October: 24.
17. 'That's not how we do things', *Times Educational Supplement,* 3 October 1986: 25.
18. O'Connor, M. (1987) 'For whom the school bell tolls', *The Guardian* 14 July: 13.
19. That's not how we do things' *Times Educational Supplement*, 3 October 1986: 25.
20. ibid.
21. ibid.

Chapter 4 – Parents in school

1. For an overview of such initiatives, see S. Wolfendale (1983) *Parental Participation in Children's Development and Education*, London: Gordon & Breach, pp. 25–32.
2. Goodacre, E. (1970) *Home and School*, Slough: National Foundation for Educational Research.
3. National Union of Teachers (1983) *Home-School Relations and Adults in the School*, London: NUT.
4. For discussions of this area see, for example, Centre for the Teaching of Reading (1983) *Parents in Partnership*, Reading: University of Reading School of Education; Hannon, P., Long, R., Weinberger, J. and Whitehurst, L. (1985) *Involving Parents in the Teaching of Reading: Some Key Sources*, USDE Papers no. 3, University of Sheffield; Topping, K. and Wolfendale, S. (1985) *Parental Involvement in Children's Reading*, London: Croom Helm; W. Bloom (1987) *Partnership with Parents in Reading*, London: Hodder & Stoughton for the United Kingdom Reading Association. Practical guides to this area include Branston, P. and Provis, M. (1986) *Children and Parents Enjoy Reading*, London: Hodder & Stoughton. Teacher trainers may find helpful Wolfendale, S. and Gregory, E. (1985) *Involving Parents in Reading: a Guide for In-service Training*, Northampton: Reading and Language Development Centre, Nene College.
5. See, for instance, Widlake, P. and MacLeod, F. (1984) *Raising Standards:*

Parental Involvement Programmes and the Language Performance of Children, Coventry: Community Education Development Centre.

6. Hannon, P., Jackson A. and Page, B. (1985) 'Implementation and take-up of a project to involve parents in the teaching of reading', in K. Topping and S. Wolfendale (eds) *Parental Involvement in Children's Reading*, London: Croom Helm, pp. 54–64.

7. Harrison, P. (1986) 'Twenty wasted years on', *Times Educational Supplement*, 2 October: 26.

8. Steirer, B. (1985) 'School reading volunteers', *Journal of Research in Reading* (UKRA), 8(1): 21–31; 'Parental help with reading in schools project', unpublished report to Educational and Human Development Committee of the Economic and Social Research Council.

9. Clover, J. and Gilbert, S. (1981) 'Parental involvement in the development of language', *Multiethnic Education Review* 3, winter/spring, reprinted in Open University (1985) *Every Child's Language*, book 2, pp. 56–60.

10. Weinberger, J. (1983) *Foxhill Reading Workshop*, London: Family Service Unit.

11. See, for example, Merttens, R. and Vass, J. (1986) 'Chorus of assent', *Times Educational Supplement*, 10 November: 47; Merttens, R. and Vass, J. (1987) 'IMPACT – a learning experience', *Primary Teaching Studies:* 263–72.

12. See Frood, K. (1986) 'Parental involvement in mathematics education: a teacher's view of IMPACT', *Primary Teaching Studies* 2(1): 95–101.

13. S. Wolfendale (1983) *Parental Participation in Children's Development and Education*, London: Gordon & Breach.

14. Torkington, K. (1986) 'Involving parents in the primary curriculum', *Perspectives* 24: 12–24.

15. S. Wolfendale, op. cit., pp. 178–9.

16. Meighan, R. (1981) 'A new teaching force? Some issues raised by seeing parents as educators and the implications for teacher education', *Educational Review* 33(2): 135–42.

17. Golby, M. (1986) 'Parental involvement: the evolution of practice', in *Perspectives* 24: 51–6.

18. Atkin, J. and Bastiani, J. (1985) *Preparing Teachers to Work with Parents – a Survey of Initial Training*, Nottingham: University of Nottingham School of Education.

Chapter 5 – Apprenticeship in the seventies

1. See, for example, Midwinter, E. (1978) *Education for Sale*, London: Allen & Unwin.

2. Mackay, D., Thompson, B. and Schaub, P. (1978) *Breakthrough to Literacy: Teachers' Manual. The Theory and Practice of Teaching Initial Reading and Writing*, 2nd edition, London: Longman for the Schools Council.

Chapter 7 – Opening the doors

1. Mackay, D. Thompson, B. and Schaub, P. (1978) *Breakthrough to Literacy: Teachers' Manual. The Theory and Practice of Teaching Initial Reading and Writing*, 2nd edn, London: Longman for the Schools Council.

Chapter 9 – Parents as helpers

1. See, for example, Tough, J. (1976) *Listening to Children Talking*, London: Ward Lock Educational.

Chapter 10 – Parents' mornings

1. Mackay, D. Thompson, B. and Schaub, P. (1978) *Breakthrough to Literacy: Teachers' Manual. The Theory and Practice of Teaching Initial Reading and Writing*, 2nd edn, London: Longman for the Schools Council.
2. Baker, A. (1985) 'Real writing, real writers: a question of choice,' in B. Raban (ed.) *Practical Ways to Teach Writing*, London: Ward Lock Educational, pp. 15–19.
3. Waterland, L. (1984) *Read With Me*, Stroud: Thimble Press.

Chapter 11 – Parents as partners

1. See, for example, Merttens, R. and Vass, J. (1986) 'Chorus of assent', *Times Educational Supplement*, 10 November: 47; Merttens, R. and Vass, J. (1987) 'IMPACT – a learning experience', *Primary Teaching Studies*: 263–72; Frood, K. (1986) 'Parental involvement in mathematics education: a teacher's view of IMPACT', *Primary Teaching Studies* 2(1): 95–101.

Useful addresses

ACE (Advisory Centre for Education), 18 Victoria Park Square, London E2 9PB.

CASE (Campaign for the Advancement of State Education), The Grove, 110 High Street, Sawston, Cambridge CB2 4HJ.

CEA (Council for Educational Advance), 79 Ellerton Road, London SW18 3NH.

NCPTA (National Confederation of Parent Teacher Associations) 43 Stonebridge Road, Northfleet, Gravesend, Kent DA11 9DS.

NAPE (National Association for Primary Education), 4 Chequers Place, Headington Quarry, Oxford OX3 2EX.

ALPAG (All London Parents Action Group), 23 Alverstone Road, London NW2 5JS.

Inner London Branch of NAGM (National Association of Governors and Managers), 22 Croftdown Road, London NW5 1EH.

ADPAG (All Dorset Parents Action Group), Worgret Manor Hotel, Wareham, Dorset BH20 6AB.

Inter-Cambridge PTAs, 201 Chesterton Road, Cambridge CB4 1AH.

Warwickshire Combined PTAs, 12 Fisher Road, Bishop Itchington, Warwickshire CV33 0RE.

PTAW (Parent Teacher Associations of Wales), Sheila Naybour, Tal Coed, Pen y Lôn, Mynydd Isa, Mold, Clwyd CH7 6YG.

References

Athey, C. (1981) 'Parental involvement in nursery education', *Early Child Development and Care* 7 (4): 353–67.

Atkin, J. and Bastiani, J. (1985) *Preparing Teachers to Work with Parents – a Survey of Initial Training*, Nottingham: University of Nottingham School of Education.

Baker, A. (1985) 'Real writing, real writers: a question of choice', in B. Raban (ed.) *Practical Ways to Teach Writing*, London: Ward Lock Educational, pp. 15–19.

Barker, R. (1987) 'Hidden factors governing the voice of parents', *The Guardian*, 24 February: 13.

Bastiani, J. (ed.) (1978) *Written Communication Between School and Home*, Nottingham: Nottingham University School of Education.

Bernstein, B. (1973) *Class, Codes and Control*, Vol.1, London: Routledge & Kegan Paul.

Bloom, W. (1987) *Partnership with Parents in Reading*, London: Hodder & Stoughton for the United Kingdom Reading Association.

Blunkett, D. (1987) 'Facing up to the new realities', *Times Educational Supplement*, 25 October: 4.

Branston, P. and Provis, M. (1986) *Children and Parents Enjoy Reading*, London: Hodder & Stoughton.

Bruner, J. (1974) *Beyond the Information Given*, London: Allen & Unwin.

Bullock Sir A. (1976) *A Language for Life*, London: HMSO.

Centre for Contemporary Cultural Studies (1982) *The Empire Strikes Back: Race and Racism in 70s Britain*, London: Hutchinson.

Centre for the Teaching of Reading (1983) *Parents in Partnership*, Reading: University of Reading School of Education.

Clover, J. and Gilbert, S. (1981) 'Parental involvement in the development of language', *Multiethnic Education Review* 3, winter/spring, reprinted in Open University (1985) *Every Child's Language*, book 2, Clevedon, Avon: Multilingual Matters, pp. 56–60.

Cullingford, C. (1985) 'Teachers, parents and the control of schools', in C. Cullingford (ed.) *Parents, Teachers and Schools*, London: Robert Royce, pp. 1–15.

Cyster, R., Clift, P.S. and Battle, S. (1979) *Parental Involvement in Primary Schools*, Slough: National Foundation for Educational Research.

David, H. (1986) 'Parent governors – elected or selected?' *Times Educational Supplement*, 3 October: 24.

Education, Science and Arts Committee (1986) *Achievement in Primary Schools*, Vol.1, London: HMSO.

Edwards, V. (1983) *Language in Multicultural Classrooms*, London: Batsford.

Frood, K. (1986) 'Parental involvement in mathematics education: a teacher's view of IMPACT', *Primary Teaching Studies* 2(1): 95–101.

Golby, M. (1986) 'Parental involvement: the evolution of practice', in *Perspectives* 24: 51–6.

Goodacre, E. (1970) *Home and School*, Slough: National Foundation for Educational Research.

Hale, J. (1972) 'Parent–teacher cooperation: an official view', in T.M. Cluderay (ed.) *Home and School Relationships*, special issue of *Aspects of Education* 15: 70–75.

Halsey. A.H. (ed.) (1972) *Educational Priority Volume 1: EPA Problems and Policies*, London: HMSO.

Hannon, P., Jackson, A. and Page, B. (1985) 'Implementation and take-up of a project to involve parents in the teaching of reading', in K. Topping and S. Wolfendale (eds) *Parental Involvement in Children's Reading*, London: Croom Helm, pp. 54–64.

Hannon, P., Long, R., Weinberger, J. and Whitehurst, L. (1985) *Involving Parents in the Teaching of Reading: Some Key Sources*, USDE Papers no. 3, University of Sheffield.

Hargreaves, D. (1984) *Improving Secondary Schools: Report of the Committee on the Curriculum and Organisation of Secondary Schools*, London: ILEA.

Harrison, P. (1986) 'Twenty wasted years on', *Times Educational Supplement*, 2 October: 26.

Herbstein, D. (1980) 'I'm in need of smalltalk', *Sunday Times*, 27 January: 12.

Hewison, J. (1985) 'The evidence of case studies of parents' involvement in schools', in C. Cullingford (ed.) *Parents, Teachers and Schools*, London: Robert Royce, pp. 41–60.

ILEA (1985) *Improving Primary Schools: Report of the Committee on Primary Education*, London: ILEA.

Jackson, L. (1974) 'The myth of the elaborated and restricted code', *Higher Education Review* 6(2): 47, 49, 65.

Labov, W. (1973) 'The logic of non-standard English', in N. Keddie (ed.) *Tinker, Tailor . . . The Myth of Cultural Deprivation*, Harmondsworth: Penguin, pp. 21–66.

Mackay, D., Thompson, B. and Schaub, P. (1978) *Breakthrough to Literacy: Teachers' Manual. The Theory and Practice of Teaching Initial Reading and Writing*, 2nd edn, London: Longman for the Schools Council.

MacLeod, F. (1985) *Parents in Partnership – Involving Muslim Parents in their Children's Education*, Community Education Development Centre, Coventry.

Maris, R. (1984) *Better Move on Frog*, London: Armada.

Meighan, R. (1981) 'A new teaching force? Some issues raised by seeing parents as educators and the implications for teacher education', *Educational Review* 33 (2): 135–42.

Mercer, L. (1981) 'Ethnicity and the supplementary school', in N. Mercer (ed.) *Language in School and Community*, London: Edward Arnold, pp. 147–60.

Merttens, R. and Vass, J. (1986) 'Chorus of assent', *Times Educational Supplement*, 10 November: 47.

Merttens, R. and Vass, J. (1987) 'IMPACT – a learning experience', *Primary Teaching Studies* 2 (3): 263–72.

Midwinter, E. (1978) *Education for Sale*, London: Allen & Unwin.

Milne, S. (1987) 'Inners and outers', *The Guardian*, 22 September: 13.

National Confederation of Parent Teacher Associations (NCPTA) (1985) *The State of Schools in England and Wales. Crumbling* schools: Fact or Fiction?; Parental Funding – How Much and What For? Gravesend: NCPTA.

National Union of Teachers (1983) *Home-School Relations and Adults in the School*, London: NUT.

O'Connor, M. (1987) 'Parent power', *The Guardian*, 31 March: 13.

O'Connor, M. (1987) 'For whom the school bell tolls', *The Guardian*, 14 July: 13.

Oram, H. (1984) *Angry Arthur*, Harmondsworth: Puffin.

Plowden, B. (1967) *Children and their Primary Schools*, London: HMSO.

Prosser, M. (1981) 'The myth of parental apathy', *Times Educational Supplement*, 16 October: 22–3.

Radin, N. (1972) 'Three degrees of maternal involvement in a pre-school program: impact on mothers and children', *Child Development*, 43: 1355–64.

Rathbone, M. and Graham, N.C. (1981) 'Parent participation in the primary school', *Educational Studies* 7 (2): 145–50.

Scottish Parent Teacher Council (SPTC) (1983) *Ideas for an Active PTA*, Edinburgh: SPTC.

Stacey, M. (1985) 'Parent/teacher partnership: from rhetoric to reality', unpublished MPhil. thesis, Cranfield Institute of Technology.

Steirer, B. (1985) 'School reading volunteers', *Journal of Research in Reading* (UKRA), 8 (1): 21–31.

Stone, M. (1980) *The Education of the Black Child in Britain*, London: Fontana.

Sutcliffe, J. (1987) 'The sleeping giant begins to stir', *Times Educational Supplement*, 20 March: 7.

Sutcliffe, J. (1987) 'Tightrope artists who have kept their balance', *Times Educational Supplement*, 17 April: 3.

Swann, Lord (1985) *Education for All*, London: HMSO.

Taylor, T. (1977) *A New Partnership for our Schools*, London: HMSO.

Tizard, B. and Hughes, M. (1984) *Young Children Learning*, London: Fontana.

Tomlinson, S. (1984) *Home and School in Multicultural Britain*, London: Batsford.

Topping, K. and Wolfendale, S. (1985) *Parental Involvement in Children's Reading*, London: Croom Helm.

Torkington, K. (1986) 'Involving parents in the primary curriculum', *Perspectives* 24: 12–24.

Tough, J. (1976) *Listening to Children Talking*, London: Ward Lock Educational.

Tough, J. (1985) *Talk Two*, London: Onyx Press.

Townsend, H.E.R. (1971) *Immigrants in England: the LEA Reponse,* Slough: National Foundation for Educational Research.

Warnock, M. (1978) *Special Educational Needs: Report of the Committee of Inquiry into the Education of Handicapped Children and Young Persons*, London: HMSO.

Waterland, L. (1984) *Read With Me*, Stroud: Thimble Press.

Weinberger, J. (1983) *Foxhill Reading Workshop*, London: Family Service Unit.

Wells, G. (1985) *Language Development in the Pre-School*, Cambridge: Cambridge University Press.

Wells, G. (1987) *The Meaning Makers: Children Learning Language and Using Language to Learn*, London: Hodder & Stoughton.

Widlake, P. and MacLeod, F. (1984) *Raising Standards: Parental Involvement Programmes and the Language Performance of Children*, Coventry: Community Education Development Centre.

Wolfendale, S. (1983) *Parental Participation in Children's Development and Education*, London: Gordon & Breach.

Wolfendale, S. and Gregory, E. (1985) *Involving Parents in Reading: a Guide for In-service Training*, Northampton: Reading and Language Development Centre, Nene College.

175

Index

44–5; partnership 45–50;
school reading 41–3; and
teachers 38–9, 47–8
parties 114–15
partnership 45–50, 157–64
assessment 159–60
further areas 158–9
learning by experience 160–1
school and community 162–3
trust 157
Plowden Report (*Children and
their Primary Schools*, 1967)
'disadvantage' 16–18, 45
home-school communications
18, 24–5, 27, 29, 83
importance of 11, 18–19, 20
PTAs 21–2, 70
policy, school 24–5
pressure groups 29–31
PTAs as 24
PTAs *see* parent-teacher
associations

race 15–16
E.P. Collier School 62–3
and events 98–9, 119
Redlands 67, 86–7, 98–9, 100,
159
reading
at home 39–41
in school 41–3; Redlands 91–2,
133–7, 138, 145–6, 159
Reading University 1, 54–5, 129
Redfern, Angela 1, 4 *see also*
Collier, E. P., School;
Redlands
Redlands Primary School,
Reading 6–7, 67–8
open-access policy 83–100
parent governors 101–11
parents as helpers 112–28
parents' mornings 129–56

partnership 157–64
PTA 69–82
Richards, Michael 68–77, 84–5,
95, 104, 117

Sallis, Joan 120
Schaub, P. 141–2
Scottish Parent-Teacher Councils
(SPTC) 24
Shearman, John 53, 55, 61, 64, 65
Smith, Frank 144
social events 73–5, 79, 80–1
sport, 120, 124
Steirer, Barry 41

Taylor Report (*A New Partnership
for our Schools*, 1977) 30, 34
teachers
as 'experts' 38–9, 47, 157
as facilitators 47
role of 162–3
training of 48
Thomas Buxton School,
Spitalfields 43
Thompson, B. 141–2
Tizard, B. 14
Tough, Joan 14, 117
trips 115, 124–5, 127
trust 157

Wade, Jill 54, 56
Warwickshire Combined PTAs
170
Waterland, Liz 145
Wells, G. 14
West Indies 15, 61
Wolfendale, Sheila 45, 46
Workers' Educational Association
(WEA) 103, 108
writing 140–3